DESIGN AND MAKE YOUR OWN
CONTEMPORARY SAMPLER QUILT

Katie Pasquini

DOVER PUBLICATIONS, INC.
New York

I would like to thank the following people:

Chris Pasquini, for his amazing drawings, and the big push; Lindsay Olsen, for his excellent color photos; Scott Ryan and Damon Maguire, for their expert advice; The Quilt Class, for their enthusiasm and wonderful quilts; Moneca, Bonnie, and Janet, for their long distance encouragement; Randi Loft, for her support and her shoulder; Lisa Berrett, for her help with the typesetting machine; Judy Donaldson, for those early morning phone calls; Terri Freedman, for putting up with me; Meeka Day, for her smiling face; Susie, for marrying my lovable brother; and Noel Watson, for occasionally taking me away from it all.

Typesetting by Katie Pasquini, Blarney Publishing, Eureka, California.
Diagrams and illustrations by Katie and Chris Pasquini.
Editing by Randi Loft, Barbara Smith, and Susie Pasquini.

To Randi & Chris and Susie. May they all live happily ever after.

Published in Canada by General Publishing Company, Ltd., 30 Lesmill Road, Don Mills, Toronto, Ontario.
Published in the United Kingdom by Constable and Company, Ltd., 3 The Lanchesters, 162–164 Fulham Palace Road, London W6 9ER.

Bibliographical Note
This Dover edition, first published in 1994, is a slightly altered republication of *The Contemporary Sampler*, originally published by Sudz Publishing, Eureka, California, in 1985. One front-matter illustration; a photograph of the author; part of the Introduction; and four blank pages headed "Notes" have been omitted. The section "Supplies" has been condensed into one page. Minor corrections have been made.

Library of Congress Cataloging-in-Publication Data
Pasquini-Masopust, Katie.
    [Contemporary sampler]
    Design and make your own contemporary sampler quilt / Katie Pasquini.
        p.   cm. — (Dover needlework series)
    Originally published: The contemporary sampler. Eureka, Calif. : Sudz Pub., c1985.
    ISBN 0-486-28197-3
    1. Patchwork—Patterns. 2. Quilting. 3. Patchwork quilts. I. Title. II. Series.
TT835.P366   1994
746.46—dc20   94-22078
                                                                                                              CIP

Manufactured in the United States of America
Dover Publications, Inc., 31 East 2nd Street, Mineola, N.Y. 11501

Front cover:
KATIE'S SAMPLER — 91" by Katie Pasquini
The trees are to remind me of the great redwoods of Northern California where I was born, the flowers are from my mother's garden, the flying geese are for my love of birds.

Back cover, left:
TWOSIES — 41" by Nancy Spruance
Twosies is my first attempt at piecing and quilting. Remembering Barbara Smith's words of advice for beginners to K.I.S.S. — Keep It Simple, Stupid, I used only the 2 patch for this sampler, and then the simplest 8 patches I could find. I always use blue and rust for learning projects. This eliminates that big decision on color. I have bags of blue and rust projects in my closet. Following Katie's design format was a real joy and was the grace that saved this from a similar destination.

Back cover, right:
IRIDESCENT EBONY — 56" by Bonnie Beck
This was my first adventure into the world of black and solid colors, and as I'm thrilled with the result, it's not likely to be my last! This quilt excites something deep down inside of me. As for the time frame, I plunged right in and devoted the next four months of my life to this quilt and amazingly enough, I finished ON TIME!! I think I'm more surprised than anyone!! (Of course, all my friends have given me up for dead. So I'm going to devote the next four months of my life to partying and making up for lost time!)

INTRODUCTION 4

SUPPLIES 5

DESIGNING 6

YARDAGE 9

TEMPLATES 14

LAYOUT 16

PIECING BLOCKS 19

MACHINE PIECING 20

HAND PIECING 22

MITERING 23

APPLIQUE 24

REVERSE APPLIQUE 27

BLIND STITCH 28

PUTTING IT ALL TOGETHER 29

BORDERS 32

COLOR PLATES 33

BASTING 41

MARKING 42

FRAMES 45

QUILTING 46

FINISHING 49

BINDING 50

HANGING 52

QUILT BLOCKS — PATTERNS — TEMPLATES 53

INTRODUCTION . . . .

This book is designed for the first-time quiltmaker, as well as the more experienced quilter who wants to try out a new format. There are three sizes of quilts: the small wall quilt, excellent for the novice as a first project because it isn't so large as to be threatening; the wall quilt, a little larger project, but still small enough for the beginner to enjoy; and the bed quilt, a larger project for those who are more ambitious. All three quilts are based on the **Contemporary Sampler Quilt** format.

This format is designed to give the sampler quilt a more contemporary look. The four center blocks allow you to see what happens when four blocks are set together without spacing. The other blocks are set off by triangle blocks and strips to enhance their individuality. By placing your own choice of blocks into the spaces provided, you design your own quilt. By choosing your fabrics, the quilt becomes even more your own statement. All of the quilts shown in the book were made by students from a class based on the format.

There is a difference in opinion as to the benefits of machine piecing versus hand piecing. It is basically a personal preference, neither is right nor wrong, just two different ways of working. I personally prefer to machine piece. With the fast pace of today's world, I think that if you begin by learning to machine piece, you may stick with it longer because you see results faster. Machine piecing can be just as accurate as hand work. This book instructs on both methods.

Quilting is a very important part of the quiltmaking process. Quilting is the stitching that holds the back, batting, and pieced top together. It is possible to do this quilting by machine, but I prefer hand quilting. I find the hand quilting a very relaxing and enjoyable activity. The difference quilting makes to the quilt is amazing, it brings life to the piece.

The most exciting time for me is binding the quilt, putting those last few stitches in and then hanging the piece on the wall and admiring what I have accomplished. I have experienced and have shared with others the excitement of a finished piece. It means different things to different people: a sense of accomplishment, pride in doing something on your own from start to finish, or making your own statement through cloth and quiltmaking.

For the beginner, I suggest following the instructions in this book step-by-step. The new quilter might be intimidated by the finished product. Just remember, it is a long process to make a quilt. Don't look too far ahead. Take each step as a short goal, a step to attaining the big goal, the finished quilt. Take it easy and relax.

For the experienced quilter, who may be just using this book for its patterns and format, use what you need from the instructions, and create your own quilt.

To all, be proud of what you create and share your accomplishments with your friends! Above all, have fun making your quilt!

Photo by Noel Watson

The Contemporary Sampler Quilt class. Front row left to right: Pam Still, Bonnie Beck, Margaret Cross, Dottie Sweet, Joyce Kelly, Bev Schmidt, Ann Seemann, Liz Miller, Bobbie McKay. **Back row:** Sue Benzinger, Cynthia Causley, Mary Ann Spencer, Lois Hansen, Edith Goggin, Jan Costley, Yvonne Thompson, Kathy Wheeler, Helen Berg, Ruth Mair, Juanette van Emmerik, Diane Huffman, Dixie McBride. **Not present:** Nancy Spruance, Joyce Eachus, Terri Freedman, Barbara Smith.

Imagine this: Tuesday evenings with 29 women — beginners to experts — surrounded by yards and yards of luscious fabrics, the sound of the exchange of ideas and laughter, and the joy of accomplishment. All of this was unified by Katie's basic design for such a versatile contemporary sampler. We were excited! It was Katie's contagious enthusiasm, sense of humor and unswerving encouragement that inspired our creations — each one so individual and personal. Thanks to Katie many new quilts now adorn our walls and beds. With this book, of which we were so fortunate and happy to be a part, many more new quilts will soften and warm the world.   Thank you, Katie, from all of us!

PENCILS —
#2 lead pencil for marking sewing lines on the light
   fabrics
White pencil for marking sewing lines on the dark
   fabrics
Water soluble pen for marking quilting lines on the
   light fabrics
White charcoal pencil or a soapstone pencil for
   marking quilting lines on the dark fabrics

RULERS —
A See-Thru® ruler with a grid marked on it
An L square or right triangle

SHARPENER — for accuracy, it is important to
keep all your marking tools sharp

TRACING PAPER — for tracing the basic format;
8½″×11″ is a good size

TEMPLATE MATERIAL — transparent plastic is
the easiest to use. It is available at craft stores with a
rough side that you can write on easily with a pencil.

SCISSORS —
Paper scissors, old funky scissors for cutting
   paper and template material
Fabric scissors, a good sharp scissor for cutting
   fabric. These should never be used for anything
   but fabric.

ROUGH SURFACE — Sandpaper or any other
rough surface for laying the fabric on to keep it from
slipping while marking around the templates. My
tabletop is an unfinished piece of plywood, which
works well.

PINS — Good quality quilter's pins; the glass-head
long pins.

SEWING MACHINE — For machine piecing any
machine that makes a good straight stitch is all that
is needed.

IRON — It is important to have an iron nearby to
press your seams as you go along.

THREAD —
Sewing thread — any good quality sewing
thread the color of your fabric or a neutral color.
Basting thread — any thread will do (preferably
contrasting in color).
Quilting thread — this is a stronger thread used
   especially for hand quilting.

NEEDLES —
Machine needles — a good needle for cotton weight
Basting needle — a long, strong needle
Quilting needles — small "betweens" made es-
   pecially for quilting; these are shorter than
   regular needles

THIMBLES — they must fit comfortably but snug.

BATTING — Any bonded batting will do. I use a 3
oz. polyester bonded batt.

QUILTING FRAME — There are many different
kinds available; I recommend the 23″ quilting hoop.

DESIGNING ....

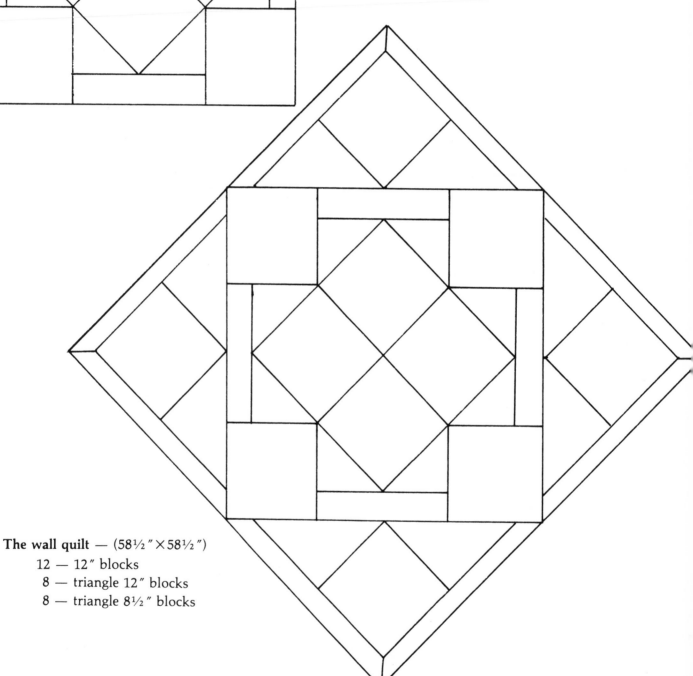

There are three different sizes of sampler quilts.

The small wall quilt — (41″×41″)
    8 — 12″ blocks
    8 — triangle 8½″ blocks

The wall quilt — (58½″×58½″)
   12 — 12″ blocks
    8 — triangle 12″ blocks
    8 — triangle 8½″ blocks

The bed quilt — (89″ × 89″)

16 — 12″ blocks

8 — triangle 12″ blocks

16 — triangle 8½″ blocks

12 — triangle 17″ blocks

DESIGNING . . . .

To design your quilt, begin by deciding which size you wish to use. (For the beginner, I suggest either wall quilt.)

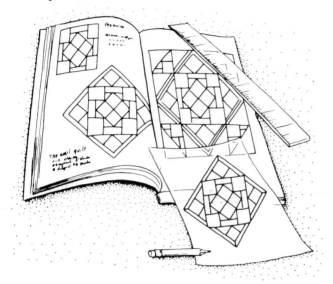

Lay tracing paper over the format you've chosen and trace it.

Then look through the patterns available in the back of the book. They are broken down into three levels of difficulty. It is better to start out with the simpler blocks for the center and as you gain confidence move on to the more difficult blocks. Lay the tracing paper over the blocks you have chosen and trace them into the blank squares of the format.

8 . . .

You may wish to use the same block pattern for the center four blocks to create an overall pattern that develops by the repeat, or four different block patterns for a different effect.

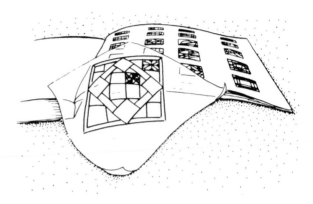

Similarly, with the outer four blocks you may wish to use the same pattern or four different patterns, or two and two.

The triangle blocks lend themselves to applique work as well as pieced work. There are patterns for these in the back also.

Once you have your sampler designed, you are ready to begin. Don't feel locked into your drawing. As you work out the first few blocks you may decide to change the next set. Let your quilt grow and change as you work.

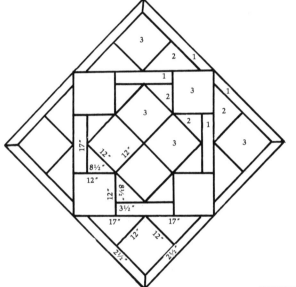

Small Wall Quilt — 41″ square

1. Strips . . . . .1/4 yd
2. Triangle blocks .3/8 yd
3. Pieced blocks . . . . .3/8 yd each of 6 fabrics
4. Backing . . . . .1-1/4 yd

Wall Quilt — 58″ square

1. Borders & strips . . . . .1 yd
2. Triangle blocks . . . . .1 yd
3. Pieced blocks . . . . .3/4 yd each of 6 fabrics
4. Backing . . . . .3-1/2 yd

Bed Quilt — 89″ square

1. Borders & strips . . . . 1-1/8 yd
2. Triangle blocks . . . . 2-1/2 yd
3. Pieced blocks . . . . .1 yd each of 6 fabrics
4. Contrasting triangles & borders . . . . . . 1-1/8 yd
5. Backing . . . . .6 yd

(Check bed for measurements
if your quilt is over 91″.)

6. Additional borders . . . . .1 yd for first border
1-1/2 yd for additional borders.

These yardage requirements are based on 45″ fabric.

YARDAGE . . . .

CHOOSING FABRICS

Choosing fabrics can be exciting as well as frustrating; it all depends on your attitude. Choose a day to go shopping when you don't have a lot of other commitments, and give yourself plenty of time so you won't feel rushed. Take a friend along and leave the kids and dog at home.

Have some idea of the colors you want to use, such as your favorite color or a specific color to match your bedroom or living room decor, but be flexible, you may find something else and change your whole plan. Wander around the fabric store until something grabs you, grab it and add to it.

Here are some ideas to keep in mind.

TEXTURE — There are two types of texture, physical and visual.

Physical texture is the actual feel of the cloth: polished cotton is smooth while corduroy is rough.

Visual texture is the look of the cloth, solids appear smooth while prints appear rough. Use different textures in your quilts to add variety. A common "rule" in quilt making is to use only 100% cotton fabrics. Although this is a good rule, (cottons are easier to work with,) I feel it is too restricting. For a bed quilt, since it will be used and laundered, I recommend using cottons, some cotton blends, and possibly some corduroy for a little texture. For wall quilts, since they will not be laundered often, anything goes; cottons and blends, corduroys and satins, and lame' for accent.

When choosing fabrics make sure to have good visual texture; small prints give the energy of the quilt, and larger prints the variety and accents, while solids give the eye a rest.

COLOR

Once you have your fabrics all stacked up, take a good look at them. Do you have a good color range from light to dark, or are they all medium? Be sure to have some light, medium and dark shades for contrast. These liven up your quilt and bring out specific parts of the design.

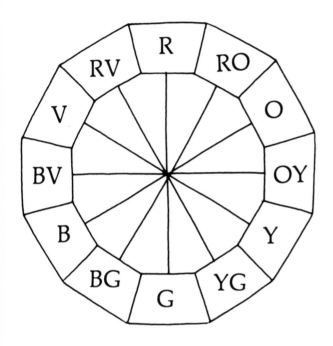

Did you choose an analogous color scheme or a monochromatic color scheme?

An analogous color scheme is one in which colors that are next to each other on the color wheel are used. Yellow, yellow-orange and orange are analogous colors. They make a very safe color scheme. When referring to temperature, these colors are known as warm colors. A good accent to use in this case would be a small amount of one of the above colors' complement; a cool color. A complementary color is the color directly opposite on the color wheel. Complementary colors for yellow, yellow orange and orange are violet, blue violet and blue.

If you have chosen a monochromatic scheme (all one color), you may wish to add an accent if it ap-

pears too dull. As above, the complementary color provides a good accent, adding life to the combination. Another good accent is that color to either side of your monocromatic color on the color wheel. For example, if you have chosen a purple color scheme, you may wish to jazz it up with its complement of yellow, or its neighbor, red or blue.

There are many possibilities, but rather than list them all and get caught up in all the technical color terms, I prefer to work with my own feelings. I call this emotional color; colors that feel good to each individual. (The personal color sense we all have.) Put out the fabrics, then study them; if you are pleased go ahead. If not, check to see if you have a good range from light to dark, good size difference (small and larger prints) and an accent or two. The most common mistake is to have all the same intensity in color and no accent.

AMOUNT

Check the yardage requirements for the size quilt you have chosen. Yardage is given for each of the different units, as well as an amount for the pieced blocks. Six fabrics should be the minimum number of fabrics used. If you want to use more than six fabrics feel free to do so, just reduce the amount of each piece in proportion to how many more than six are added. For example: If you want to use 8 different fabrics, instead of buying 3/8 yd of 6 different fabrics which equals about 2 yards total, you would only need 1/4 yd of 8 fabrics, which equals 2 yards also. If you want to use more than 8 fabrics do so, but 1/4 yd is the smallest amount of yardage you should buy. Anything smaller is too hard to work with.

When cutting the yardage, get separate pieces for each item. Cut one piece for borders and strips and cut one piece from the same fabric for the pieced blocks. Label them as such.

Preshrinking the yardage is advisable, especially for bed quilts, which will need to be laundered. Wash lights and darks separately.

When making the bed quilt be aware that you may need extra fabric to border it out to the right size. The bed quilt measures 89" across. Add strips to the outside edge until the quilt is large enough to fit your particular bed.

YARDAGE . . . .

For the first-time quilters who think that picking the colors that "feel good" is somewhat obscure, if not intimidating, here is Chris' basic guideline for picking a color scheme that looks good and is harmonious.

One sure way to have a harmonious quilt is to pick a similar (analogous) color scheme as mentioned before, such as red with its analogous colors, red-orange and red-violet. This gives you three of your six fabrics.

For an accent, you could pick one of your basic color combination's complements. In this case it would be blue-green, green or yellow-green. To really be effective as an accent you need to use just a small amount. One way to assure this is to only use the compliment in the pieced blocks. You now have four of your six fabric colors.

By now, you have your design in outline form on your tracing paper. Where you put your darks, lights and medium colors affects how your design will come out as shown above. You may find it helpful to pencil in your contrasts on a second piece of tracing paper over your design. Use solid for dark colors, lined for medium and leave the light colors blank. This will show you the contrast of your block and possibly help you pick contrasting fabrics.

So far, you have worked with individual blocks, making choices on contrast and putting accent color in them. Now these blocks will be shown off in the overall quilt by how you choose color contrasts for the triangle blocks and the strips. Using one light solid material for the triangle blocks will help tie the quilt together and provide a background for the pieced blocks and strips. It also will allow intricate quilting to show up. If dark colors are used for the strips, they will pull the pieced blocks together into a total design on top of the light background.

Now, armed with a color scheme and contrast drawings, it is time to go to the store to pick your fabric. The chart at the bottom of this page may help you in your selection. The numbers after the fabrics in the chart refer to the placement of the fabric in the bed quilt design below. If you are doing one of the wall quilts just ignore parts not applicable to your design.

In the color scheme chart below, any three adjoining colors on the color wheel can be substituted for either of the analogous color schemes. Then pick one of their three complementary colors and you will have a harmonious color scheme.

If you do use this chart, the yardage you need for each fabric is calculated for you in the accompanying amount chart.

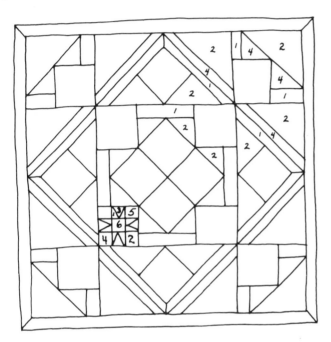

YARDAGE CHART

	Small Wall Quilt	Wall Quilt	Bed Quilt
1	5/8 yd	1 3/4 yd	2 1/8 yd
2	3/4 yd	1 3/4 yd	3 1/2 yd
3	3/8 yd	3/4 yd	1 yd
4	3/8 yd	3/4 yd	2 1/8 yd
5	3/8 yd	3/4 yd	1 yd
6	3/8 yd	3/4 yd	1 yd

Analogous Color Scheme #1	Variation #1	Variation #2
Red-Orange	Dark (print) (1) Light (print) (4)	Light (solid) (2) Light (solid) (4)
Red	Medium (print) (3) Medium (print) (5)	Medium (print) (3) Medium (print) (5)
Red-Violet	Light (solid) (2)	Dark (print) (1)
Complement — yellow-green or green, or blue-green	Medium (print) (6)	Dark (print) (6)
Analogous Color Scheme #2	Variation #1	Variation #2
Blue-green	Medium (print) (3) Light (solid) (2)	Medium (print) (3) Light (solid) (2)
Blue	Dark (solid (5)	Dark (print) (1)
Blue-Violet	Medium (print) (4) Dark (print) (1)	Dark (solid) (5) Medium (print) (4)
Complement — yellow-orange or orange or red-orange	Light (print) (6)	Dark (print) (6)

TEMPLATES ....

To make an accurate quilt, you must begin with accurate templates. The more you make, the more accurate you will become. Begin by being very careful when making the templates, then everything else will fall into place.

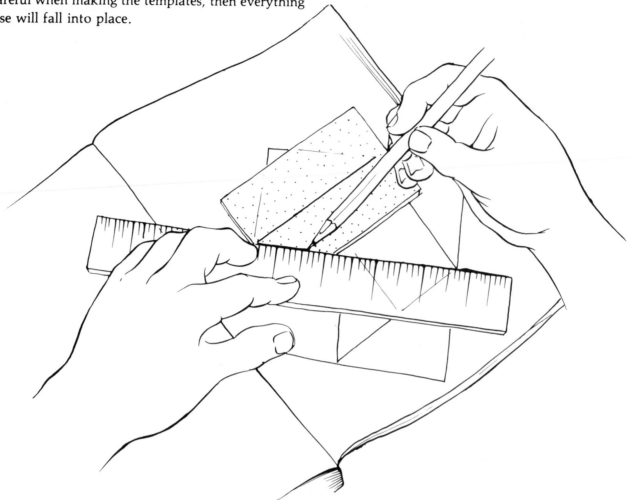

There are two ways to make templates. There are templates without a seam allowance, and those with a seam allowance. I find it more accurate for machine piecing to use templates without the seam allowance added.

To make the template, place the frosted plastic over the patterns in the back of the book, frosted side up. Using a sharp pencil and a ruler, trace the pattern onto the plastic.

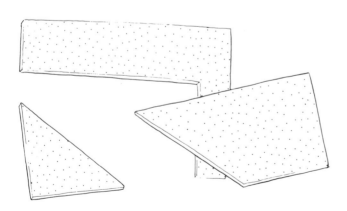

Lay the template upside down on the back of the fabric and trace around it. This line is now the sewing line.

A lot of the templates will be interchangable between blocks within each grouping, so label each template with its grouping (2 patch, 3 patch, 6 patch, etc.) and its name.

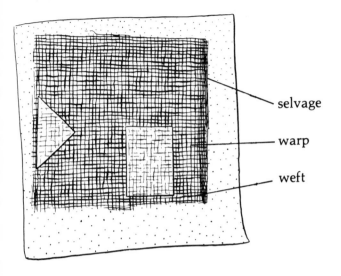

selvage

warp

weft

You will need to add a seam allowance. 1/4″ is the allowance used in quilt making. This seam allowance may be added by measuring and drawing 1/4″ larger than the seam line. A see-through ruler with lines 1/4″ apart is perfect for this.

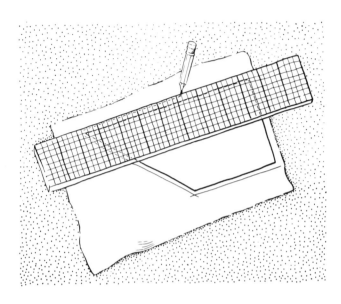

When laying the template on the fabric, you need to be aware of the grain lines. These are the lines or threads that run in two directions making up the fabric, the warp (which is parallel to the selvage), and the weft. Be sure to line the template up square with these lines. For triangles, place the long side on the grain (warp or weft).

If you find your fabric slipping as you mark around the templates, you may need a rougher surface on which to work. A large sheet of fine grain sandpaper will do or a piece of unfinished plywood.

Or you may wish to eyeball (cutting 1/4″ out from the sewing line). Once you are familiar with the 1/4″, it will become easy to eyeball.

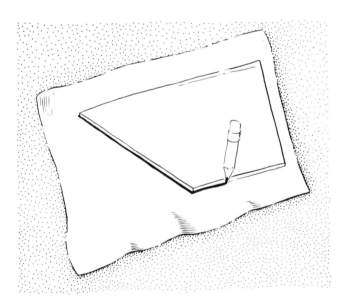

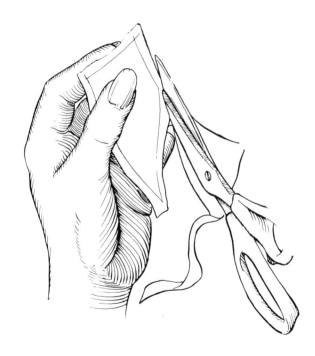

LAYOUT . . . .

Strips, borders, and triangle blocks need to be cut from the designated pieces. Using a ruler and triangle or L square, draw the sewing lines onto the fabric in the manner illustrated below.

Place the L square or triangle on the selvage edge of the fabric. This will assure you that your sections are square. Leave space between pieces in order to add the 1/4″ seam allowance. This can be done by measuring 1/4″ larger or by eyeballing when cutting. Any leftover fabric can be used in the pieced blocks.

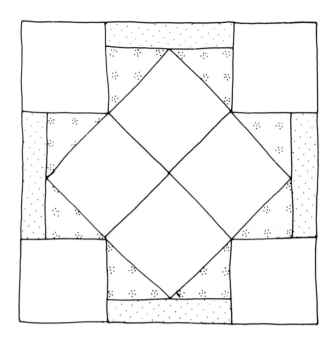

SMALL WALL QUILT

Strips

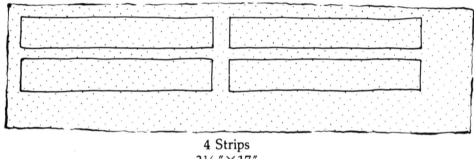

4 Strips
3½″×17″

1/4 yd

Triangle blocks

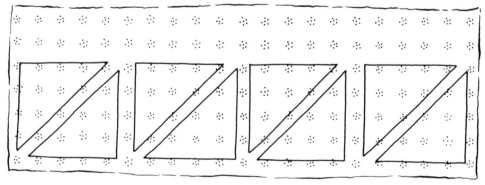

8 Triangle blocks
8½″×8½″

3/8 yd

WALL QUILT

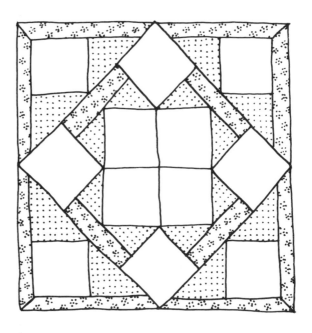

Borders & Strips

8 Borders — 30″ × 2½″
4 Strips — 3½″ × 17″
_____
1 yd

Triangle Blocks

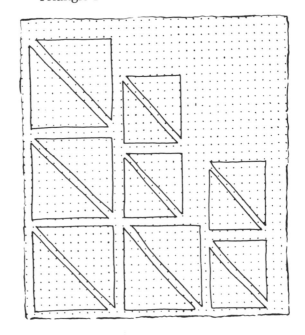

8 Triangle blocks — 12″ × 12″
8 Triangle blocks — 8½″ × 8½″
_____
1 yd

LAYOUT . . . .

BED QUILT

Borders and Strips

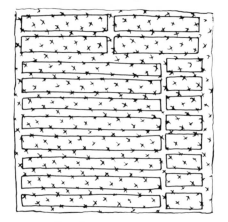

8 Borders — 2½″ × 30″
4 Strips — 3½″ × 17″
8 Strips — 3½″ × 8½″

1 1/8 yds

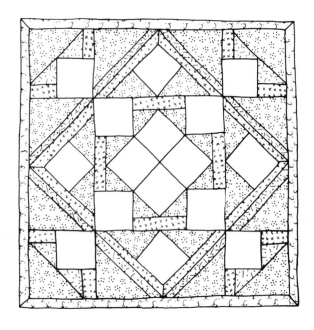

Triangle Blocks

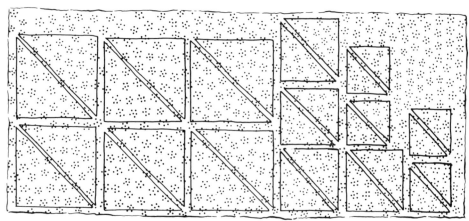

12 Triangles — 17″ × 17″
8 Triangles — 12″ × 12″
8 Triangles — 8½″ × 8½″

2 1/2 yds

Contrasting triangles & borders

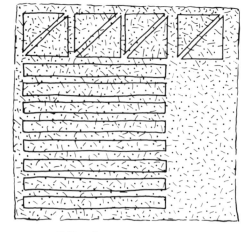

8 Borders — 30″ × 2½″
8 Triangles — 8½″ × 8½″

1 1/8 yds

Additional Borders

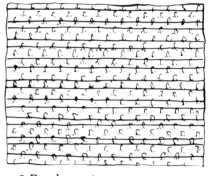

8 Border strips — 3½″ × 44″

1 yd

After choosing the block, making the templates, and cutting out the fabrics, you will need to put them together to form the block.

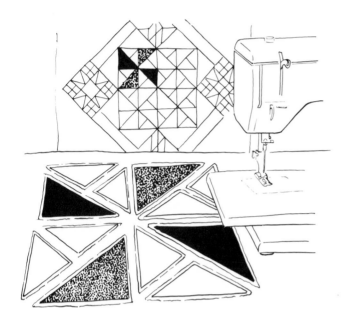

The easiest way to see the sewing order for each block is to break it down into units (2 patch, 3 patch, etc.) Find out what is needed to complete each unit, then sew the smaller units together to form larger units. Begin by laying the fabric pieces in the proper order near the sewing machine. Sew the units together, being careful to follow your designated pattern.

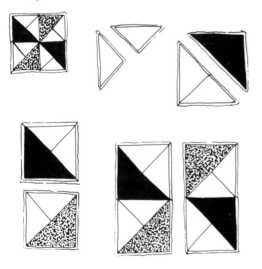

For example: This block is from the 2 patch; there are two units on a side. Each unit is made up of two

smaller units, triangles. Sew the two triangles together to form the squares, then sew two squares together to form two rows. Sew the two rows together to complete the block.

This block is from the 3 patch; there are three units on a side. Each pattern is made up of smaller units, in this case two different sets are used. One consists of four small squares, and the other of three triangular units. Sew each unit together first to form the squares, then sew the squares together in rows, and lastly sew the rows together to complete the block.

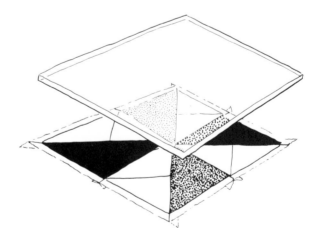

The finished block should measure 12½ " (this includes two seam allowances). Make a master template out of cardboard that measures 12½ " square. Lay this over the block and trim away any excess.

MACHINE PIECING . . . .

For machine piecing, a good straight stitch is all that is needed. Accurate pinning is an important part of good machine piecing.

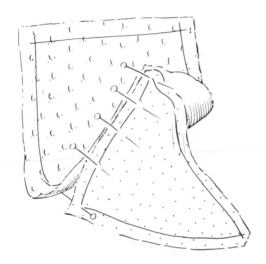

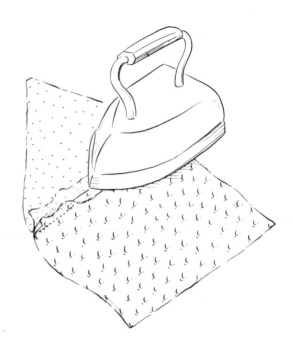

Straight Seams — For straight seams, line both pieces up so the sewing lines match. Place a pin in the corners. Be sure the pin is on the line on both pieces. Pin perpendicular to the line with the head of the pin to the outside. Depending on the length of the seam, pin between the two corner pins to assure there will be no slipping.

Press seams open as you go for wall pieces and to one side for bed quilts. (The reasoning behind this is that for bed quilts pressing to one side makes the seams stronger and for wall quilts pressing them open makes a crisper, more accurate line, although slightly weaker.)

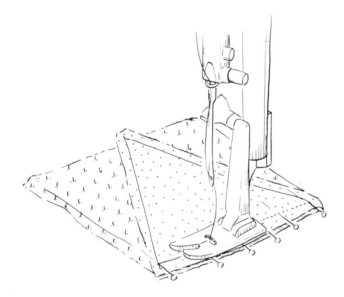

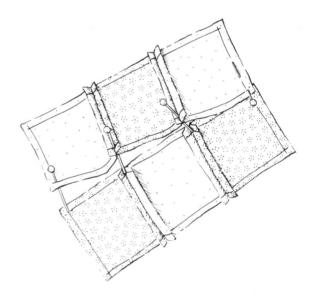

Sew on the marked line from one edge to the other. Because these seams will be crossed by another seam there is no need to back stitch on the straight seams. (Note: this rule changes for corner seams.)

When sewing units or rows together, be sure seams match. Do this by pinning the lines and seams together. Sew right on the line crossing the pin where it goes into the line.

Corner Seams — Corner seams should be treated as two straight seams. Line one side up, pinning corners and between.

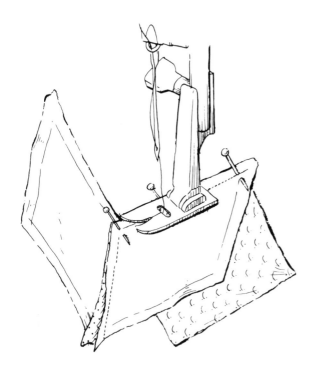

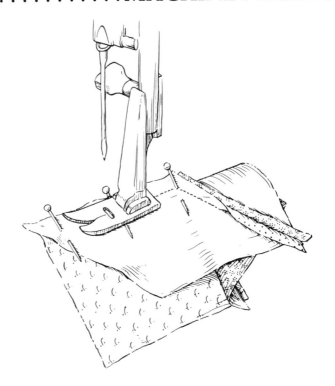

Sew from outside edge to inside corner, stopping right at the pin with one backstitch to hold. Do not go further than the end of the seam line. If you do, the fabric will not lie flat when turned.

Turn the fabric, pin the corners and start sewing exactly at the inside corner with a backstitch, sewing to the edge.

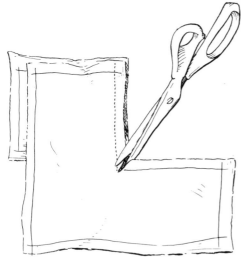

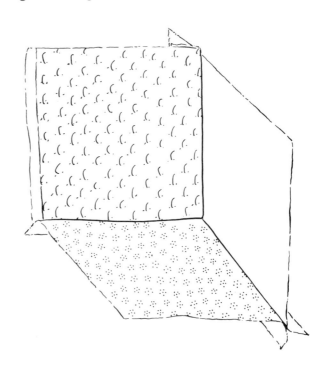

If the inside corner is made up of one L-shaped piece as above, clip the corner after sewing the first straight seam to allow the fabric to turn.

When you open this up, your corner should lie flat. If not, check to see if you clipped in all the way to the line, and that you have sewn exactly on the sewing lines.

HAND PIECING ....

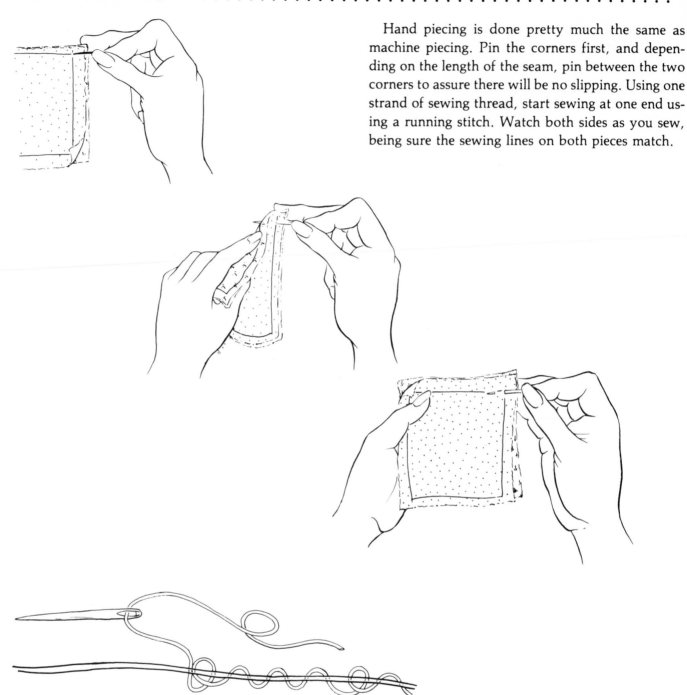

Hand piecing is done pretty much the same as machine piecing. Pin the corners first, and depending on the length of the seam, pin between the two corners to assure there will be no slipping. Using one strand of sewing thread, start sewing at one end using a running stitch. Watch both sides as you sew, being sure the sewing lines on both pieces match.

Every four or five stitches take a little backstitch to strengthen the seam. These seams should be pressed to one side for both wall and bed quilts for added strength.

Mitered corners give a very professional look to
the corners of the quilt.

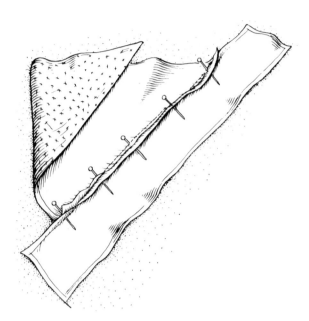

To miter, begin by sewing a border to the main
unit, leaving at least as much excess beyond the corner equal to the width of the border. For example, if
the border is 3″ leave at least 3-1/4″ excess. Be sure
to stop sewing 1/4″ from the edge of the main unit.
(Sew with the main unit on top, the border
underneath.)

Fold the entire unit on the diagonal from the corner. The borders should lay directly on top of each
other. Using a ruler extend the diagonal line made
by the fold through the borders. This becomes the
sewing line. Sew on that line, starting the seam
directly on the inside point where the two previous
seams end. Trim the excess to 1/4″ and press open.
This should leave you with a nice flat mitered
corner.

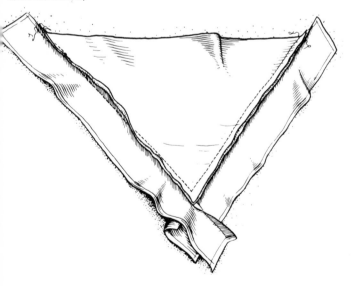

Sew another border to the other side being careful
not to catch the first border in the seam, and stop
1/4″ from the edge of the main unit.

APPLIQUE . . . .

Templates for applique work are made the same as for pieced work, except for the marking.

Instead of marking on the wrong side of the fabric, as you do for piecing, mark on the right, or topside, so you can see where to turn the seam allowance under. Then cut out, eyeballing 1/4″ larger.

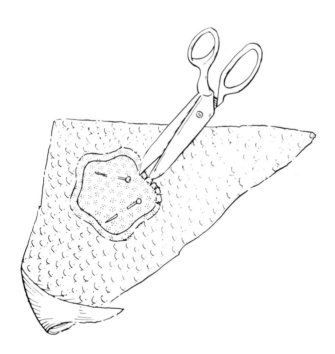

Position the applique on the block and pin or baste in place. Make perpendicular cuts to the sewing line every 1/4″. Do only a few inches at a time. One stitch per clipped area is sufficient. Continue to fold under the clipped pieces and stitch in place.

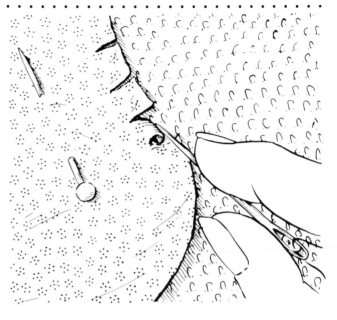

Use one strand of sewing thread the same color as the applique. Knot the thread and pull it through from behind. Hold the work in your left hand, sewing counterclockwise (reverse for left handed.) Use the needle to fold under the clipped seam allowance until the seam line is turned under.

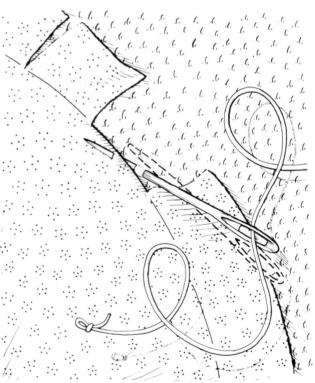

Take a blind stitch to secure the turned-under fabric. The stitches should be into the fold so they won't show.

Applique should be done in block form before the quilt is all pieced together.

For outside points, stop clipping 1/4″ from the point. Clip 1/4″ from the point on the other side. This will leave an arrow-like point to be turned under.

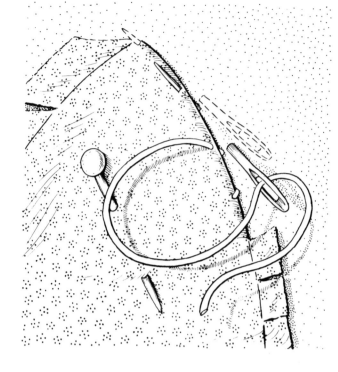

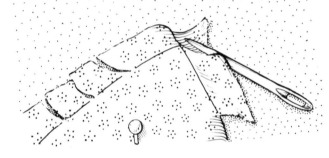

Do this by first turning the point under and holding it in place with your thumb.

Take a stitch in the middle of the clipped portion you have just turned under, then a stitch in the point.

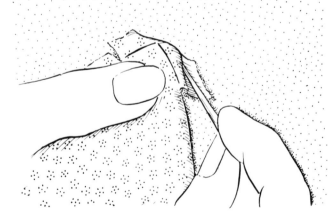

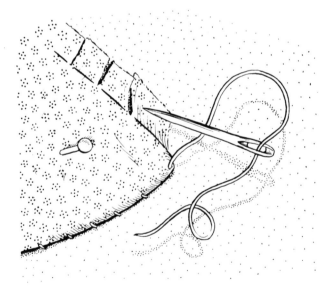

Turn the right side under and hold it in place with your thumb also.

Turn the fabric around in your hands and turn under the other side; take a stitch and continue appliqueing.

APPLIQUE ....

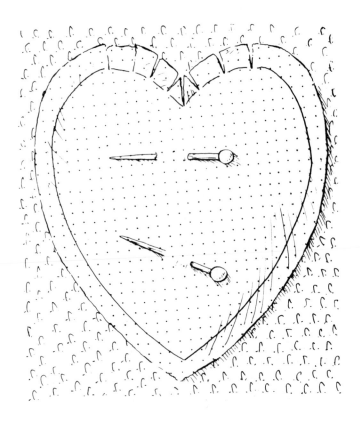

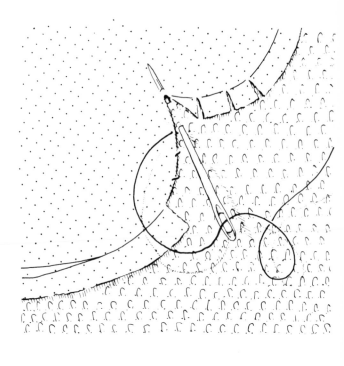

Inside points need to be clipped right to the center in order to make a sharp point.

Before turning under the left side, take a stitch right in the center.

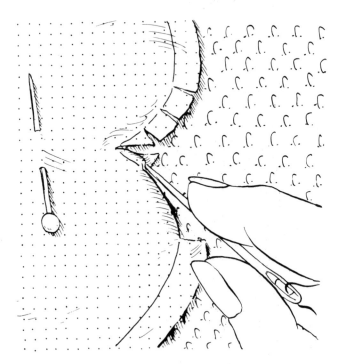

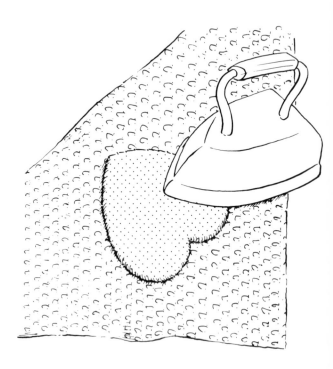

Turn under the right side and stitch in place.

Turn under the left side, stitch and continue on. For all applique work press flat once the whole piece has been sewn down.

Reverse applique templates are made the same as applique templates. The difference between the two is the surface marked.

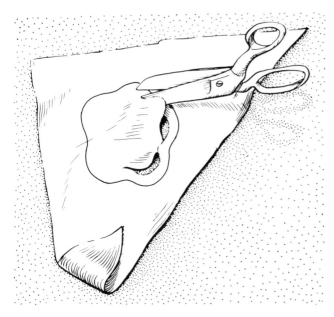

The background fabric is marked and trimmed rather than the piece to be appliqued. For example, when working with a flower, mark the sewing line onto the background fabric, cutting 1/4″ inside the line.

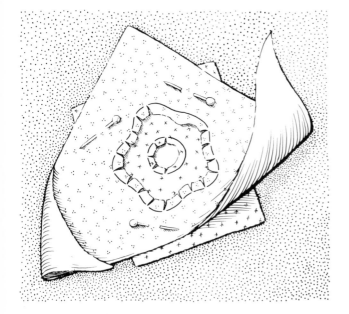

Choose the flower fabric, cut a piece large enough and place it behind the hole. Pin or baste it in place.

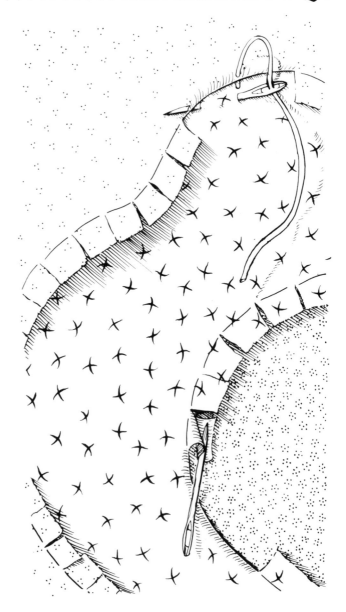

Clip and blind stitch the seam allowance under to reveal the flower. For the center of the flower, mark the circle onto the flower, cutting away the center. Place a center fabric behind the flower. Clip and blind stitch the seam allowance. When you have finished, the layering will be just the reverse of the applique. Trim any excess fabric from behind and press.

Both appliques work well. As a general rule, it is easier to reverse applique small pieces and circles, and applique larger units.

BLIND STITCH . . . .

The blind stitch is used for applique and finishing
bindings and hems.

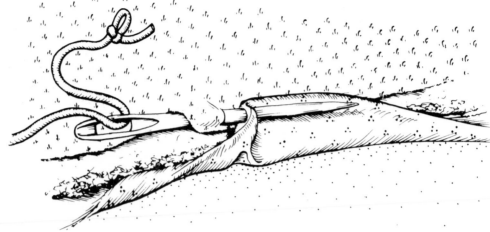

Begin by knotting the thread and hiding the knot under the applique or binding.
Insert the needle through the under fabric. Bring the needle up through the edge of the fabric sewn.

Insert the needle back into the under fabric directly next to where the needle just came out; this leaves
only a small amount of thread visible.
Continue until done.

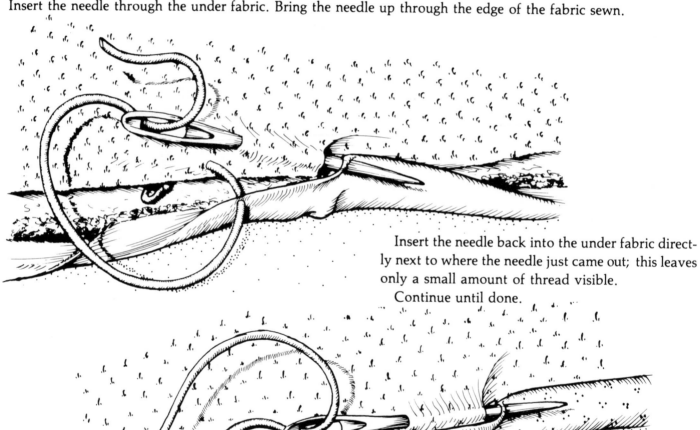

Start in the center and work your way out.

Once the blocks are constructed, you need to set them with the strips and spaces.

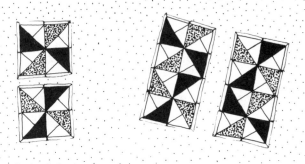

Sew the four center blocks together to make one large square.

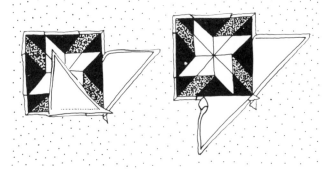

Next, sew two 8-1/2″ triangle blocks to the second set of pieced blocks. With right sides together pin the short side of the triangle block to the pieced block.

Sew from the inside corner to within one inch of the end of the right angle on the triangle block. Repeat this on the other side. This will allow you to piece in the 17″ strip with ease. (Note: if your pieced block is a directional one, i.e., a basket or a tree, be sure to sew the triangle blocks to the proper side to insure the block will sit right on the quilt.) Repeat this with the other triangle block.

Sew these units to the four center squares.

Now sew the 17″ strip lengthwise to the straight seam line formed by the triangle blocks. This leaves the ends of the strips and the unsewn inch of the triangle free. With right sides together, sew these free ends. This will complete the small wall quilt.

. . . 29

PUTTING IT ALL TOGETHER . . . .

Next, sew the outer borders on, mitering the corners. (See mitered corners pg 23.)

The wall quilt is made by adding a large triangular unit to each side of the small wall quilt, and then adding a border.

To make this triangular unit, sew two 12" triangle blocks to the third set of pieced blocks.

Sew these units to each side of the small wall quilt piece. Repeat with each side, and you have the wall quilt.

Sew a 2-1/2" by 30" border to the long side of a 17" triangle block, centering the border, leaving equal amounts of excess at either end. Press. Using a ruler, draw a line that extends the straight edge of the triangle block. Trim on this line.

The bed quilt is an extension of the wall quilt by the addition of a larger triangular unit to each of its sides, with an additional border.

Sew these to the square, giving you a larger triangular unit.

For the bed quilt, sew an 8-1/2" triangle block to a 3-1/2" by 8-1/2" strip. Sew two of these to the pieced block.

Next sew on a 17" triangle block to complete the square.

Sew this larger triangular unit to the existing unit. Add on outside borders to finish the bed quilt.

BORDERS . . . .

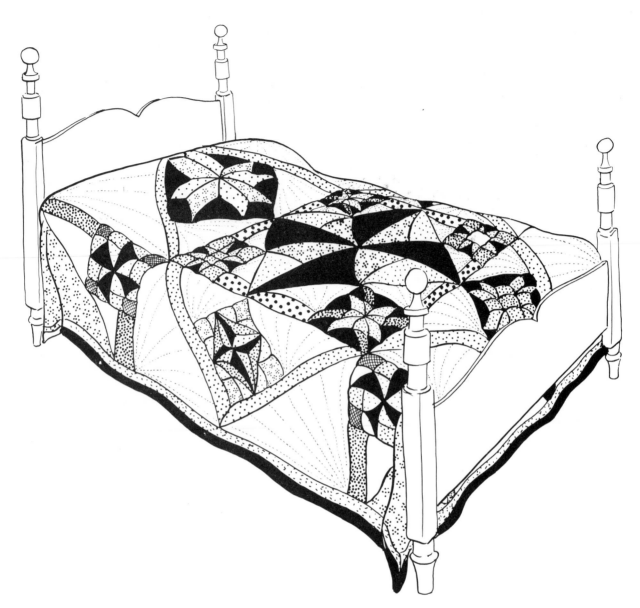

You may need to add borders to bring it to the right size for your bed.

To do this, cut strips the length of the quilt plus two times the width of the strip. For example, if the length of the quilt is 89″ and the border is 3″, cut the strip 95″ (89″ plus 2 × 3″ equals 95″). You will need to piece strips to get the full length. Cut lengths as shown in the layout and sew them together. Trim to the desired length. Sew the strips onto the bed quilt, mitering the corners.

This will make the quilt 95″ square. Measure the bed this quilt will fit and see if it is large enough. If not add a second set of borders. These should be 95″ plus 2 × 3″, which equals 101″. Sew these on, mitering the corners. Continue adding until you reach the desired size.

BED SIZE QUILTS		
Bed Size	**Quilt Size**	**3″ Borders**
Full Size Coverlet	89″	Main Border
Full Size Spread or Queensize Coverlet	95″	1 Additional Border
Queensize Spread	101″	2 Additional Borders
Kingsize Coverlet	107″	3 Additional Borders
Kingsize Spread	113″	4 Additional Borders

Be sure to measure your particular bed and adjust the number of borders and their width accordingly.

Plate 1 **A TISKET A TASKET** — 48″ by Dixie McBride

I took this class because my machine and I seem to be enemies. I wanted to see if I can solve this problem. When I learned it was to be a sampler class, I wanted to back out of the class because I'm not crazy about samplers until I saw the design format, then it became interesting. My first blocks were far from perfect, but as I progressed, I seemed to get better with the machine. The more I did, the better I got. I liked the idea of having a finished top so fast, I think I'll do some more machine piecing.

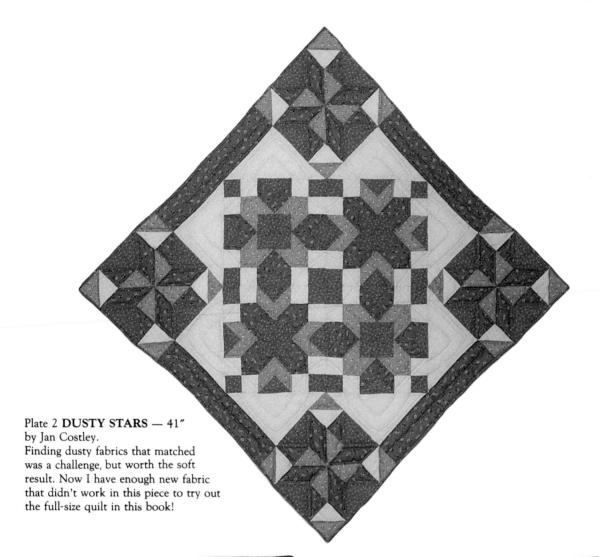

Plate 2 **DUSTY STARS** — 41″
by Jan Costley.
Finding dusty fabrics that matched
was a challenge, but worth the soft
result. Now I have enough new fabric
that didn't work in this piece to try out
the full-size quilt in this book!

Plate 3 **AUTUMNAL PATCHES** — 41″ by Helen Berg
The ease and speed of machine sewing gave me the incentive to
complete my wall hanging. I used the suggested yardage; I don't
think I would be comfortable purchasing any less. An error might
make you search for a pattern that had been "sold out".

Plate 4 **NEW DIRECTIONS** — 41″ by Sue Benzinger
This quilt is not just another fabric project, but is part of a deeper
process of change and maturity. I am discovering a creative outlet
through stitchery, and can see many new directions for this energy.
Although I've never made a quilt before, I found the whole process
in this format to be challenging, without being overwhelming. I'm
really happy with the end result and proud to have successfully tried
something brand new.

Plate 5 **PHOENIX** — 41″ by Kathy Wheeler
Trying this new sampler layout, I decided to use color and texture combinations that were experimental. I chose the colors and center pattern, then rearranged the colors in all the different combinations within that block. The center blocks finished so strong, I was lost coming up with the next four blocks. Finally (for lack of any better solution), I picked a simple block similar to my center and repeated the central colors.

Plate 6
PLAINLY AMISH — 48″
by Juanette van Emmerik
I found this format a great challenge for me, as it gave me an opportunity to combine my favorite elements of a traditional Amish quilt and come out with a design all of my own. The most difficult part for me was, "becoming one with my quilt." Though I joked that my piece was "deaf-mute," once it did start to "talk" things flowed much faster and I was much more satisfied with my decisions.

Plate 7
NANCY'S CHOICE — 53½"
by Lois Hansen
I chose corner post in the brown and
rust tones because it almost matches the
beveled glass doors on either side of the head-
board of Nancy's old-fashioned oak bedroom suite.
The green eight-pointed stars are a good contrasting
color.

Plate **8 COUNTRY VIEW** — 62" by Pam Still
Your first idea of what you think the quilt will be is not always
how it turns out. Your ideas are constantly changing, but when
the last piece is sewn on — it all seems right!

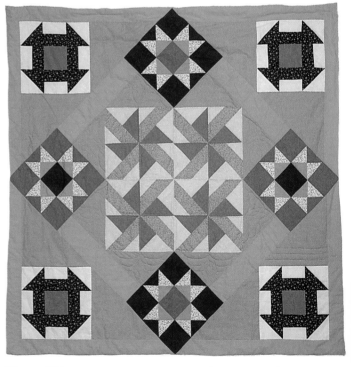

Plate 9 **OLD-TIMELY PASTELS** — 60" by Yvonne Thompson
This was my first effort with the machine. It was much easier to
be precise than I thought. This format is a wonderful change
from the traditional sampler. My favorite part was deciding
which four squares to put in the center. The edges of these
squares butt up together to form a new central design.

Plate 10 **STONE MASON'S NIGHTMARE** — 57″ by Ruth Mair
This quilt was machine pieced and machine quilted. I had no serious problems other than keeping the back from bunching up as I machine quilted. The experience has been unparalleled.

Plate 11
GATHERING FLOWERS — 67″
by Diane Huffman
I like the idea of using Katie's format to
make a patchwork quilt, because, as a beginner, I
would have been too intimidated to attempt it on
my own. I enjoyed it!

Plate 12
PURPLE MAIZE — 56″x74 ″
by Margaret Cross
I learned many technical skills
from this project, but, more
critically, I understand now
the importance of balancing
the darks and lights in the
overall design. It is difficult to
forsee the consequences of
your actions when you are
hunched over several different
fabric scraps and an array of
tiny templates. I can't wait to
start my next quilt so that I
can put this knowledge to
use!

Plate 13 **SALUTE THE HARVEST** — 41″
by Mary Ann Spencer
My quilt is constructed of four-patch blocks. The deep rich
colors in the baskets and the stars symbolize the bountiful
California harvest.

Plate 14 **BABY DREAMS** — 40″ by Liz Miller
The best advice I can give to someone planning a quilt like this is
to not get hung up with one idea. Ideas are not cement. Play
with your design. It will evolve wonderfully. If you find
yourself frustrated with an idea, color or a specific block, be
willing to change. You and your quilt will grow from it.

Plate 15 **PURPLE HAZE** — 41″ by Bobbie Mckay
I found that as soon as I began quilting my piece, I became
obsessive about my work. It would take nothing short of an
earthquake to move me from my chair, much to the dismay of
my three-year-old son. As soon as he would see me with my
sewing basket he'd exclaim, "Oh no! Are you quilting again? We
better not bug mom!"

Plate 16 **INLAID CORDUROY** — 42″
by Cynthia Causley
After our first class session I knew I was hooked. Little did I
know that working on a wall hanging was going to consume
most of my waking hours when I wasn't at my regular job. Now
that the piece is complete and looks just right in the room it was
made for, I feel a real sense of accomplishment.

Plate 17 ORANGE SURPRISE — 90″ by Joyce Eachus
It was so exciting! As you complete each section, you're happy with what you've got, but when you add the next step you're surprised with the difference. It will hang on my son's living-room wall.

Plate 18 ALIKI — 84″ by Ann Seemann
I approached this quilt with a mental attitude of experimentation, including all aspects from design, to color selection, to assembly, to quilting patterns. Having been accustomed to cutting out quilt pieces with an exact ¼″ seam allowance, I was skeptical about using Katie's technique. But I was instantly rewarded with the precision that came in assembling complicated blocks (that I had previously avoided).

Plate 19 WITH LOVE TO KIRSTIN — 91″
by Bev Schmidt
My granddaughter, Kirstin, graduated from high school in June and this is her graduation gift. I am making quilts for all fourteen grandchildren as they graduate. Thanks to Katie, I have more confidence in tackling this task. Machine piecing will make construction go faster.

Plate 20 SHADES OF BLUE — 68″
by Edith Goggin
Shades of Blue was my first machine piecing project, which to my surprise was fast and fun. Thanks to Katie's class, I plan to make another.

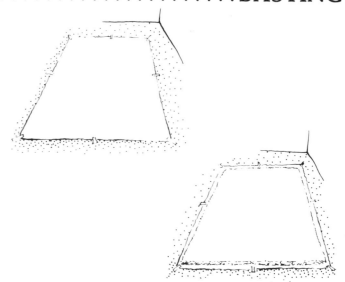

The pieced top, the batting, and the backing are what make up the quilt. Basting holds the three layers together while you quilt. The backing is one piece of fabric. For the small wall quilt one length of backing is all that is needed. A length is one width of the fabric (44"–45") by the length of the quilt plus a few extra inches for safety. For the wall quilt and bed quilt two lengths are needed to get the full width. Sew the two lengths together and press the seam open. (At this point, you need to read over the types of marking for quilting you might prefer. Some types need to be marked before the basting is done.)

Lay the backing, right side down, on the floor and tape in place.

Lay the batting on top of the backing.

Finally, lay the pieced top on the batting, right side up. Tape the top in place also. Using a long needle and single thread, start basting in the middle, taking large stitches through the three layers and stitch to the outside edge. Do this in a radiating manner all around the quilt. For the wall quilts, add basting around the outside edge. The bed quilt will need rows in the middle and outside edge. The backing and batting should be a few inches larger than the top. Trim excess if necessary.

MARKING . . . .

There are two ways of marking your quilting patterns or designs: mark all the lines before you baste and quilt, or mark each block as you are ready to quilt it. I find that the easiest way is to mark them as you get to them. The traditional way to quilt is to stitch 1/4″ from each seam line. A more contemporary way is to use the seam line as a suggestion for the quilting line. If the square has a diagonal seam line you could possibly quilt a diagonal line in the opposite direction, or quilt lines that echo the set of a pattern.

Traditional
Quilting Pattern

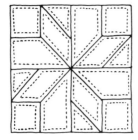

Following a suggested seamline
as a quilting pattern

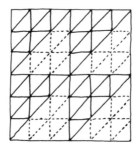
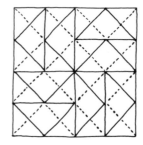

Crossing a diagonal seamline
as a quilting pattern

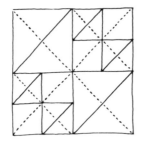

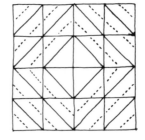

Echo Quilting
Patterns

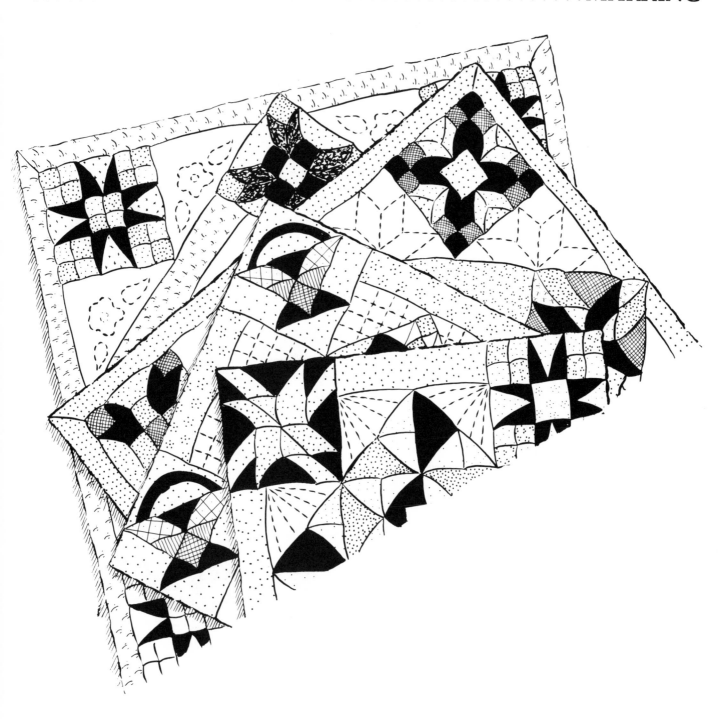

If you have made the triangular blocks of solid material, you will be able to do a lot of quilting to enhance them. You can use the applique patterns in the back of the book as quilting patterns. One could quilt a grid onto the triangular blocks or quilt the outline of one of the pieced blocks. A radiating pattern would be another possibility. The ideas go on and on. Play with it and have fun.

Keep in mind that intricate quilting patterns will show up much better on solid fabrics; prints seem to hide the stitching.

MARKING . . . .

weight paper. An ice pick can be used to make holes for the pattern.

Using foam rubber or a rug as a cushion, punch holes every ¼", following the drawing.

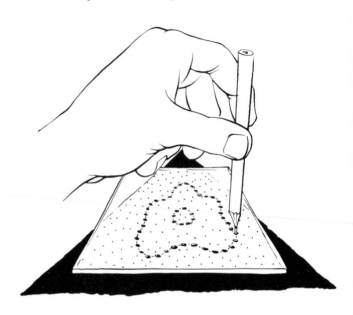

To mark patterns onto light fabrics, simply trace them. Outline the pattern on paper with a black felt marker. Lay the quilt over the pattern and trace it using a fabric pencil. (Be sure to test to make sure that the pencil you use will come out later.) This type of marking needs to be done before the quilt is basted.

Place this template on the fabric and, using a sharp fabric pencil, mark through the holes onto the quilt.

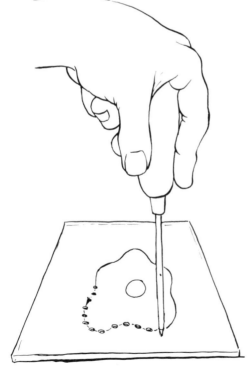

To mark dark fabrics, you will need to make a template. Do this by drawing the pattern on heavy

Remove the template and remark the design.(There are also commercial templates available with areas punched out for marking.)

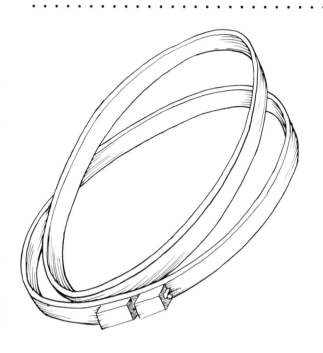

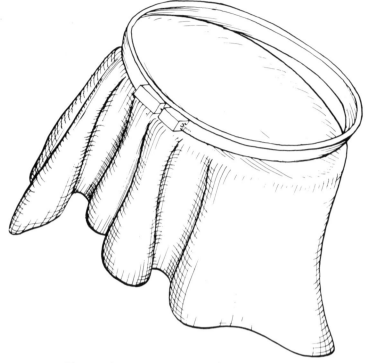

Now that you are ready to start quilting you will need a quilting frame. There are various frames available: the large floor frame which holds the entire quilt, the square lap frame, and the round hoop. I recommend the 23" round hoop because a 12" block will fit inside it, making it easier to quilt one block at a time.

Always begin working from the center out. Start by placing the inside ring of the hoop under your piece, then place the loosened outside ring on top and push down over the inside ring. Stretch evenly and tautly, then tighten the outside ring.

Before you begin stitching, turn the hoop over, making sure there are no wrinkles on the back side. If there are, stretch them out.

Needle & Thread

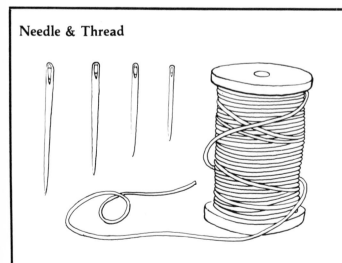

There are special needles for quilting called "betweens." The smaller the needle, the larger the number.

Begin with size 9, gradually working your way down in size to a 10, then a 12. The smaller the needle, the smaller the stitches.

Thread your needle with about 12 to 18 inches of quilting thread. Be sure to use quilting thread as it has been waxed to make it stronger. Choose a color that will blend with your quilt. You may wish to change the color of the thread depending on the color of the block. If quilting thread is unavailable in the color you want, pull regular thread across beeswax to strengthen it.

QUILTING . . . .

Quilting is a series of small running stitches, the purpose of which is to hold the three layers of cloth together. It creates texture and dimension and should enhance the design.

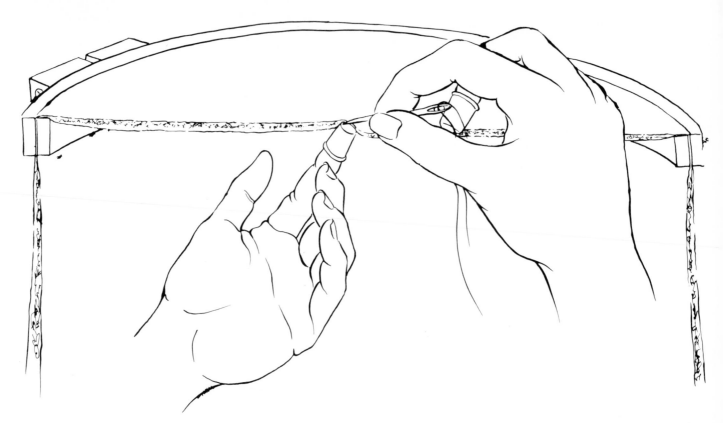

The needle goes up and down through the fabric to produce this running stitch. There are many ways to do this.

I work from the top, using two thimbles, one on the middle finger of my right hand to push the needle through the fabric; the other on the index finger of my left hand under the fabric.

Set the quilting hoop on your lap. Push the bottom thimble hard against the quilt in the spot you wish to stitch, making a ridge. Put the needle into the ridge, letting go of the needle with the index and thumb. Using the pressure of the thimble against the needle, push through, glancing off the bottom thimble coming up through the quilt. Repeat. (I do this one stitch at a time, making as small and even a stitch as possible.)

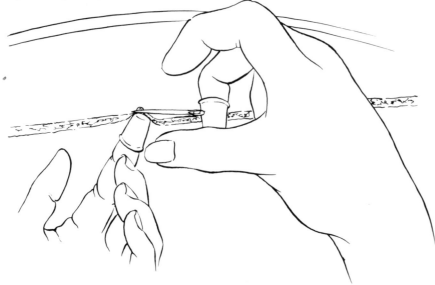

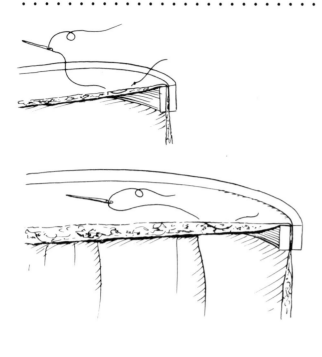

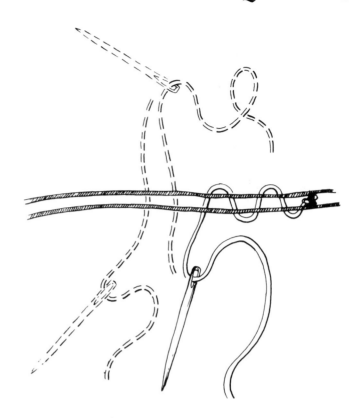

It is important not to have the knot show on either the back or the front of the quilt. The knot should be hidden between the layers. To start quilting, insert the needle between the layers about one inch from where you plan to start. Pull the needle through at the starting point and gently tug the knot to the inside.

Other ways of quilting include the stab stitch. Stab the needle through the fabric and pull it out through the bottom, stabbing the needle back up and pulling it through, on and on, one stab at a time.

Another quilting technique is the running stitch. Put several stitches on the needle before it is pulled through. It is all a matter of personal preference; find which way works best for you.

Backstitch to end a line of quilting. Take two stitches, one on top of the other, piercing through the thread of the backstitch to help secure it, then hide the end between the layers. Clip the excess thread.

QUILTING ....

Start quilting in the center of the quilt. After quilting the center, move the hoop out, working your way around the quilt.

When you reach the outside edge, baste on a piece of muslin. This will allow you to continue to use the hoop and keep the tension even.

Some feel it is very important to have very tiny stitches. For beginners, I think it is more important to have even stitches. As you get more comfortable with quilting, your stitches will get smaller and smaller.

To finish the quilt you need to enclose the edge. There are two ways to do this.

One is to fold the backing over to the front. Trim the backing so there is about a 2" excess all the way around. Trim the batting to 1" excess.

Fold the backing edge over 1/2" for the hem, then fold again to the front and blind stitch.

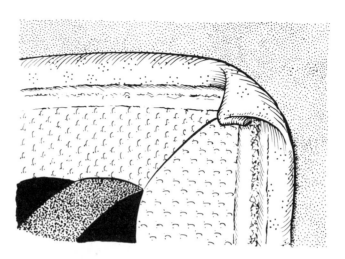

For the corners, make a mitered corner by folding both sides in for a hem, then fold the corner point directly in on the diagonal.

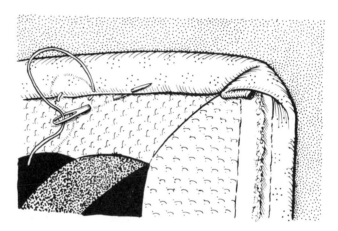

Fold each side in the second time to get the mitered corner and blind stitch.

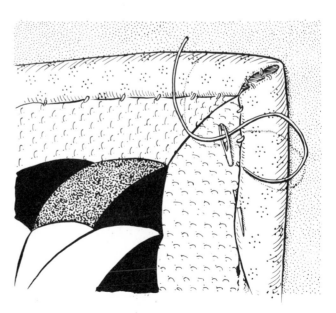

BINDING ....

The other way to finish the edge is to bind it with a bias binding.

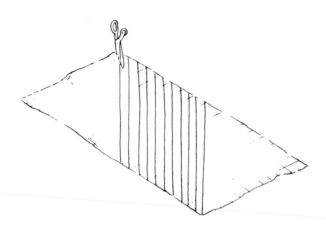

One half yard will make plenty of binding for the wall quilts, one yard for the bed quilt. Cut 2″ bias strips. Find the bias by folding the fabric on the diagonal, matching the adjacent straight edges. Mark the two ends. Using a ruler make lines 2″ apart following the bias edge. Cut these strips and sew them together to form one long bias strip.

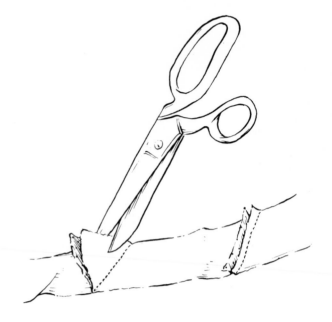

Trim away the excess leaving only 1/8″, press seams open.

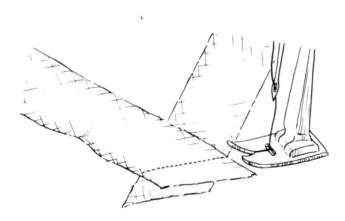

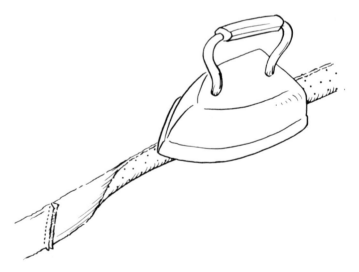

Press the long strip in half, wrong sides together.

To do this lay two strips, right sides together, so they form a 90° angle on the end. The actual seam will be on the straight of the grain of both pieces.

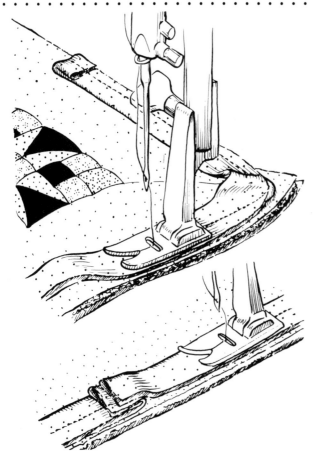

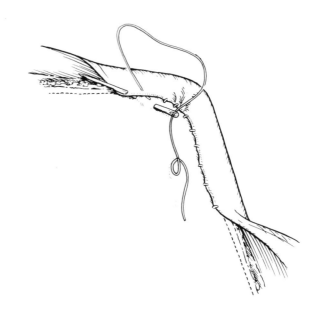

To finish the binding, simply roll folded edge of bias to the back and blind stitch into place.

Sew the bias to the front of the quilt, with both of the open edges next to the raw edge of the quilt. To start, fold the end of the bias up approximately 1/4″ to form a finished edge. Machine stitch with a 1/4″ seam allowance, easing the bias around corners. (It is important not to stretch the bias as you sew, stretching will cause the quilt to curl.)

Finish sewing the binding by placing the end over the folded bias. Trim any excess binding.

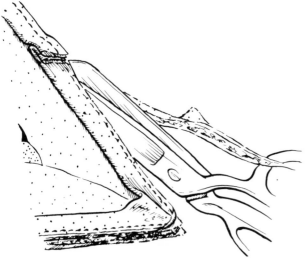

Signature

To make it "official", sign and date your finished quilt. This can be done by embroidering on the front or the back, or by cutting a small rectangle of muslin and writing or typing on it. Sew this to the back of your quilt.

Trim seam allowance to 1/8″ through all layers, including the bias strip, quilt top, batting, and backing.

HANGING . . . .

A sleeve should be sewn onto the top of the quilt so it can hang on a wall (or in a show!).

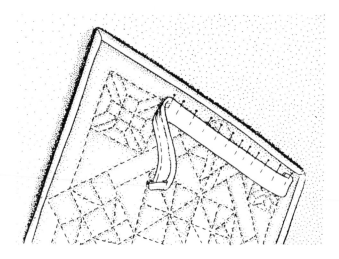

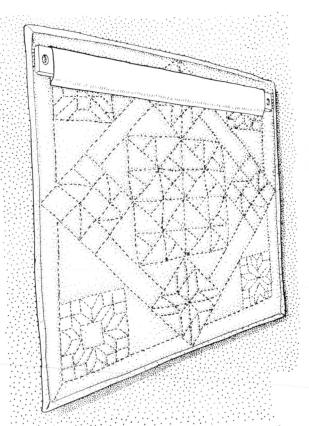

Make a sleeve out of the excess backing or a piece of muslin. Cut the strip 4″ wide and as long as the top of the quilt. Fold the ends and the edges under 1/2″ and press.

Lay the fabric sleeve along the top edge of the quilt, about 1 inch from the side edge. Using a blind stitch, sew the sleeve along the top edge, about 1/2″ to 1/4″ from the top edge. Then sew the bottom of the sleeve in place.

A pole can be inserted through the sleeve to hang it.

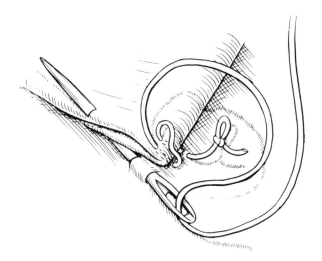

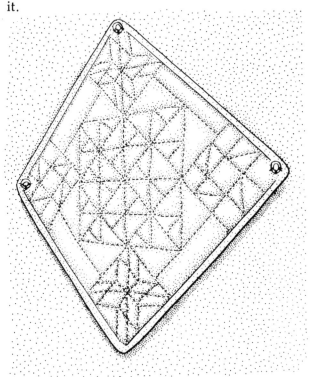

For the wall quilt that hangs on the diagonal, 1/2″ curtain rings are used. Small plastic rings are sewn to the top point and the two corners. Use small nails or tacks to hang it to the wall.

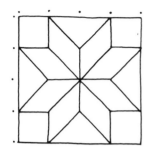
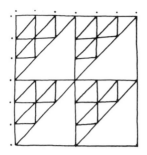

Each page of blocks is divided into beginner, intermediate and advanced blocks. If this is your first quilt you may wish to use the beginner's blocks. As you progress and gain confidence you might try the more difficult blocks. Take it slowly at first.

Once you have designed your quilt on tracing paper, you are ready to make the templates. First you need to find the right patterns. The patterns for each grouping are on the pages following the actual blocks. Each pattern is the finished size (without seam allowance). There are little diagrams along each combination of patterns. These will help determine the right template for your block. Take the tracing paper design and center the block you are making templates for over the little diagrams, find the one that matches the shape and size you are looking for. Locate that pattern in the combination of patterns and make a template. (See templates, pg. 14.)

There are over 130 quilt blocks and their patterns on the following pages. The blocks are grouped according to the number of patches along any given side, as follows: Two patch, Three patch, Four patch, Five Patch, Six patch, and those not fitting into any category.

Each block has little dots along the top and down the left side, these let you know which grouping it is from. Count the number of spaces between the dots to determine the number of patches. A patch can be one square or it could be broken down into triangles, squares, diamonds, etc. It doesn't matter how many pieces each patch is made up of, the type of block is determined by the number of main patches.

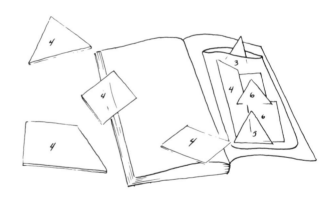

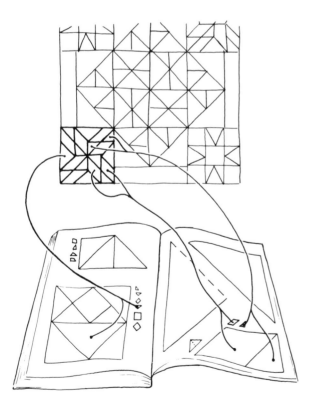

Label the templates with the grouping (two patch, three patch, etc.). Some templates will be interchangeable between blocks and groupings. You may want to label the template with the name of the blocks it is used for also.

A manila envelope or a Ziplock bag stapled to the back of the book makes a convenient place to store the templates.

2 PATCH

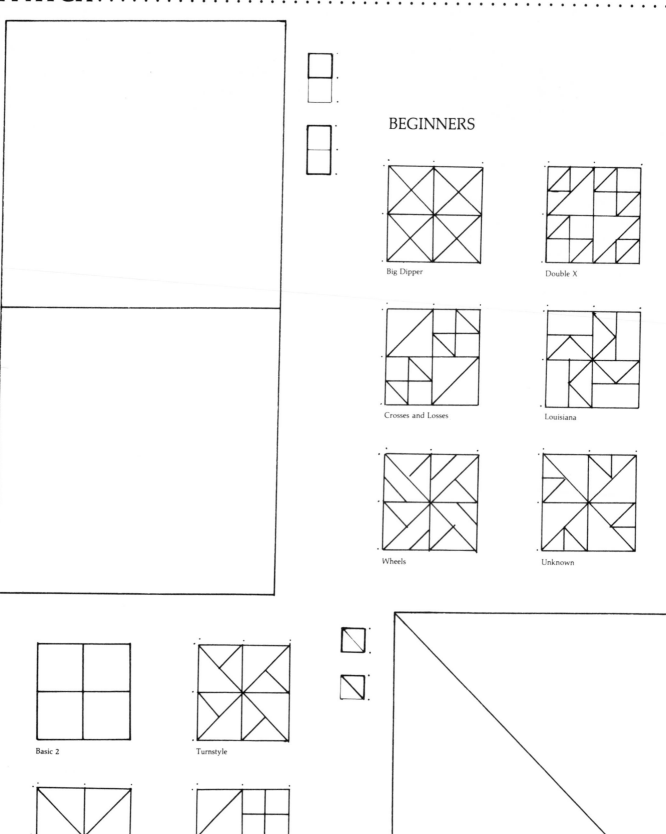

BEGINNERS

Big Dipper

Double X

Crosses and Losses

Louisiana

Wheels

Unknown

Basic 2

Turnstyle

Wind Mill

Northern Star

INTERMEDIATE

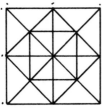

Unknown 4 patch

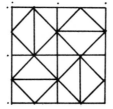

Next Door Neighbor

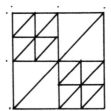

Flock of Geese

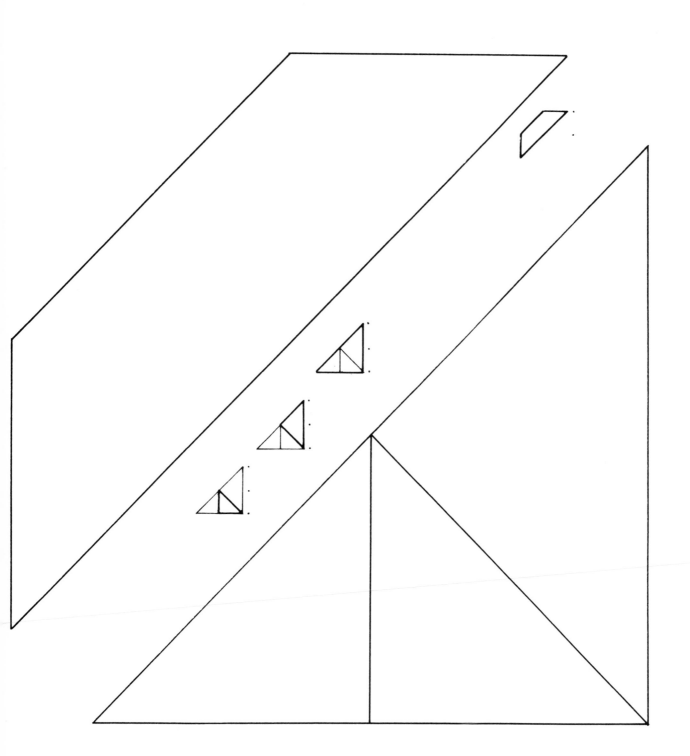

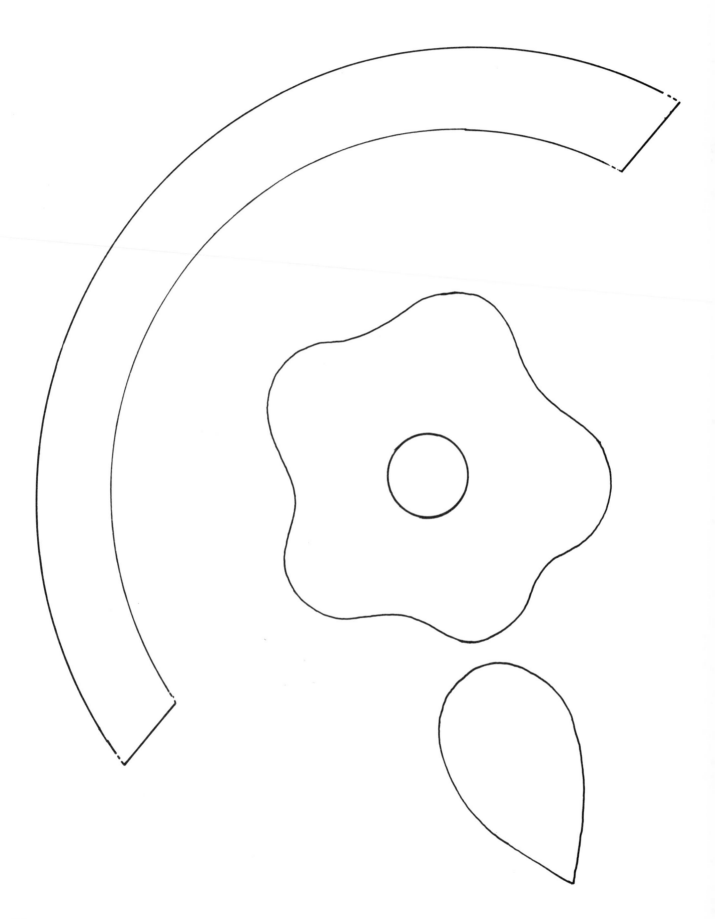

BEGINNERS INTERMEDIATE ADVANCED

Basic 3

Unknown

Rolling Stones

54-40 or Fight

Winged Square

Shoo fly

Palm Leaf

Letter X

Card Tricks

8 Pointed Star

Double X

Morning Star

Prairie Queen

Capital T

Cat's Cradle

Friendship Star

Texas Star

Weathervane

Rocky Road to California

Weathervane variation

Contrary Wife

Churn Dash

Water Wheel

Album

Katie's Block

Cypress

Jacob's Ladder

Unknown

Sawtooth Patchwork

Ann's Block

Sun Rays

Variable Star

Goose Tracks

Unknown

Blocks and Star

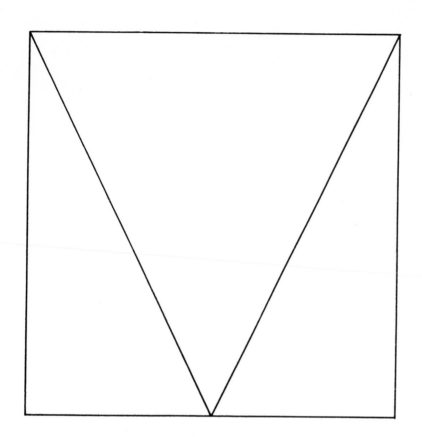

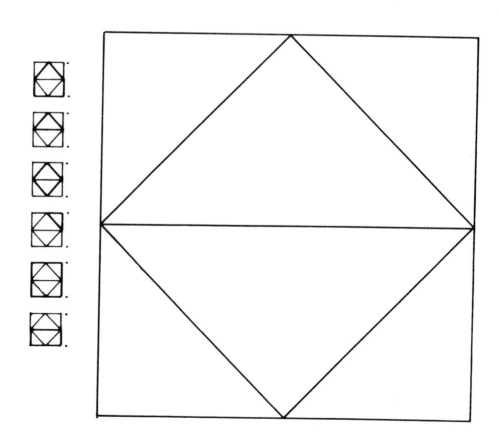

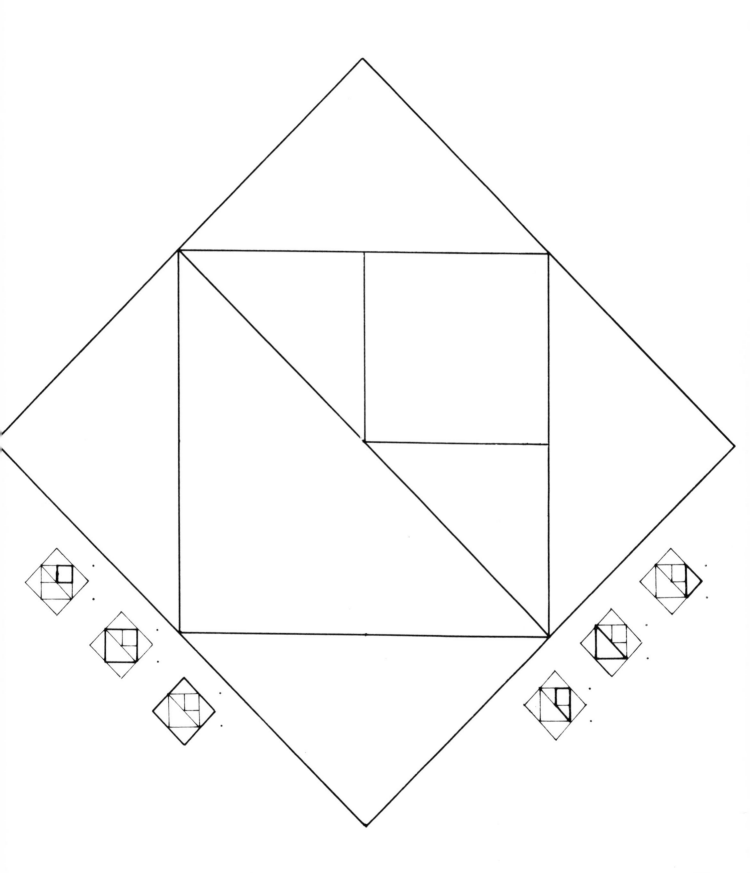

APPLIQUE HEARTS . . . .

BEGINNERS   INTERMEDIATE   ADVANCED

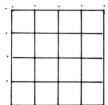

Basic 4

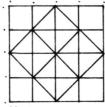

Mosaic

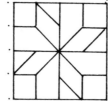

Clay's Choice

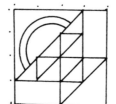

Basket

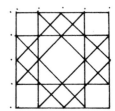

Georgetown Circles

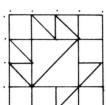

Road to Oklahoma

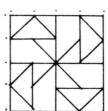

See Saw

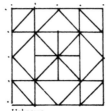

Whirligig

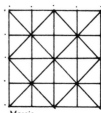

Unknown

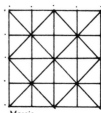

Mosaic

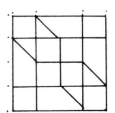

Basket

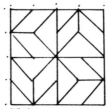

Louisiana

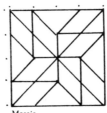

Mosaic

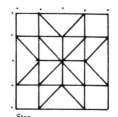

Star

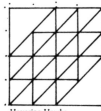

Hovering Hawks

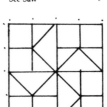

Nelson's Victory

Windblown Square

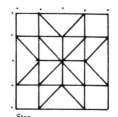

Flower Basket

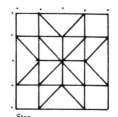

Star

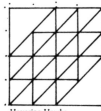

Bulkan's Puzzle

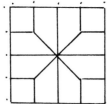

Cactus Basket

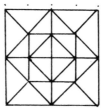

Shooting Star

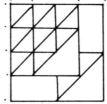

Nelson's Victory

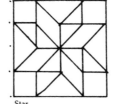

Columbus

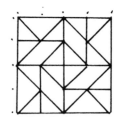

Bachelor's Puzzle

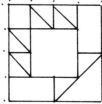

Scrap Zigzag

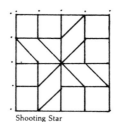

Unknown

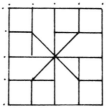

Evening Star

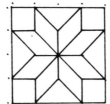

Basket of Diamonds

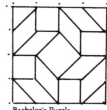

Road to Paris

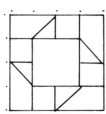

Pinwheel

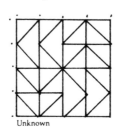

Dutchman's Puzzle

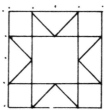

Hourglass

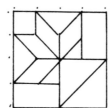

Shooting Star

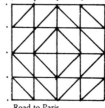

Old Tippecanoe

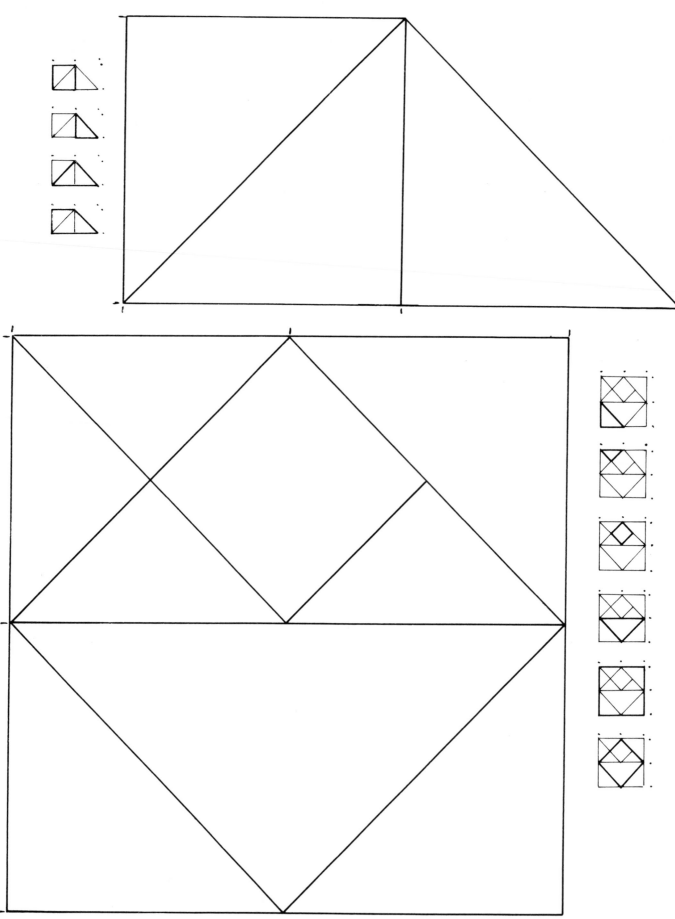

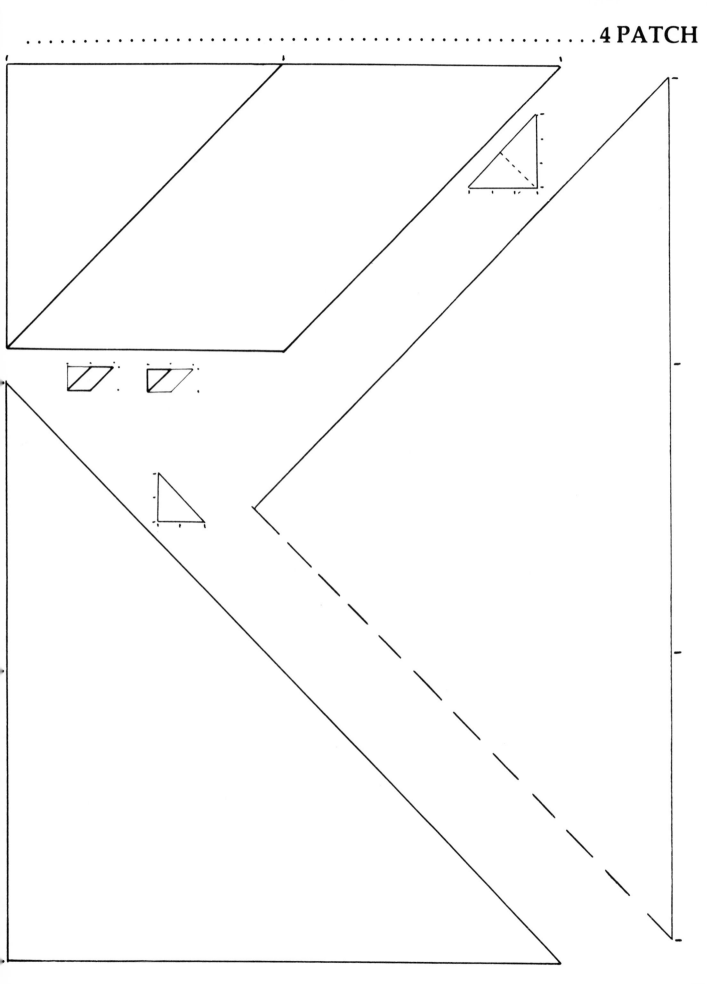

APPLIQUE FLOWERS ....

BEGINNERS

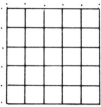

Basic 5

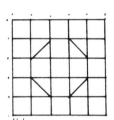

Unknown

Sisters Choice

Double Wrench

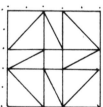

Crazy Ann

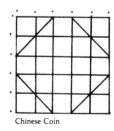

Chinese Coin

INTERMEDIATE

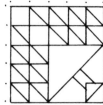

Temperance Tree

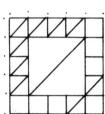

Fruit Basket

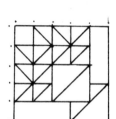

Fruit Basket

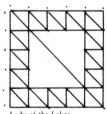

Lady of the Lakes

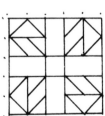

Jack in the Box

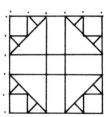

Signal

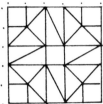

Pinwheel Square

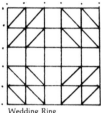

Wedding Ring

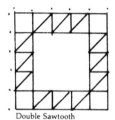

Double Sawtooth

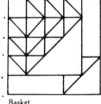

Basket

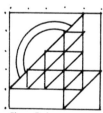

Cherry Basket

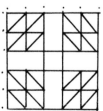

Handy Andy

ADVANCED

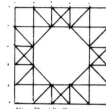

King David's Crown

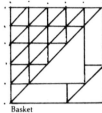

Basket

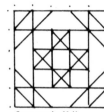

Square and a Half

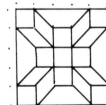

Corner Posts

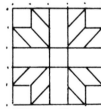

Wild Rose and Square

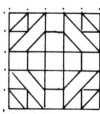

Gem Blocks

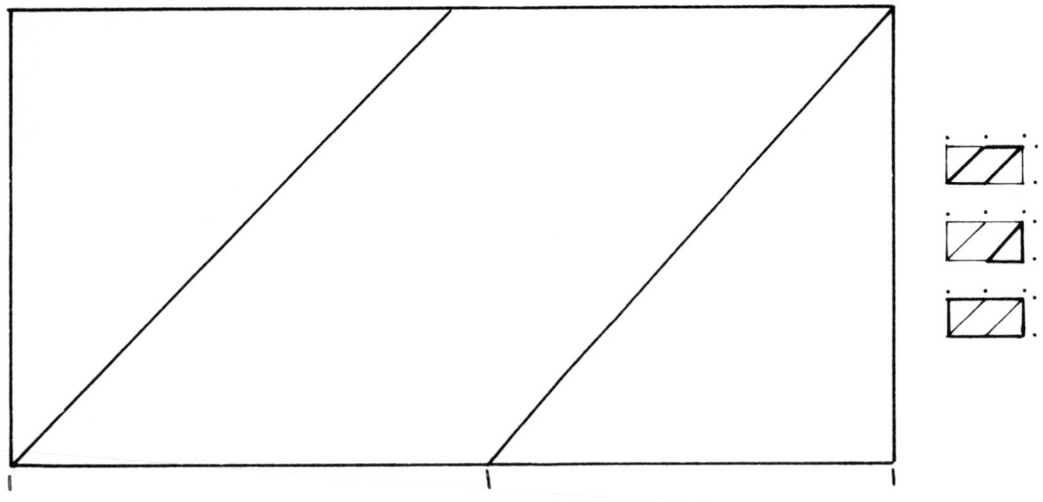

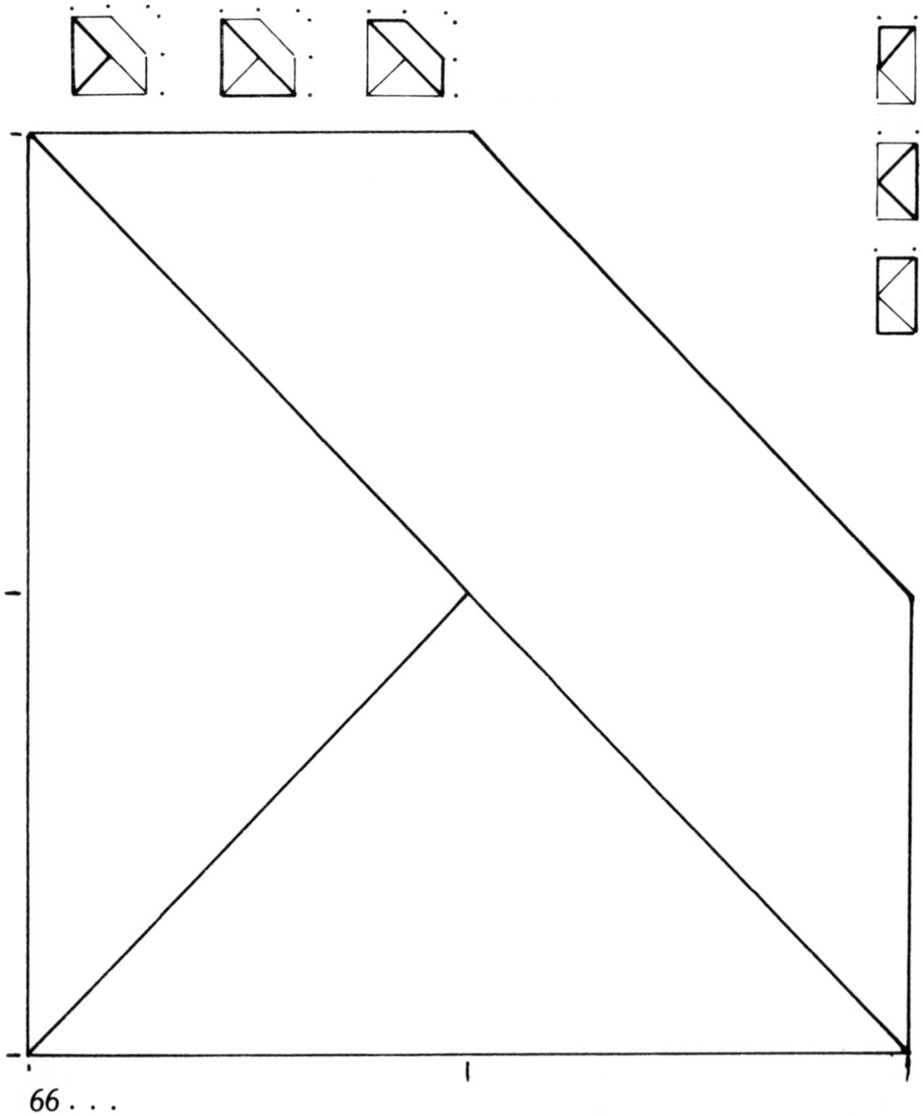

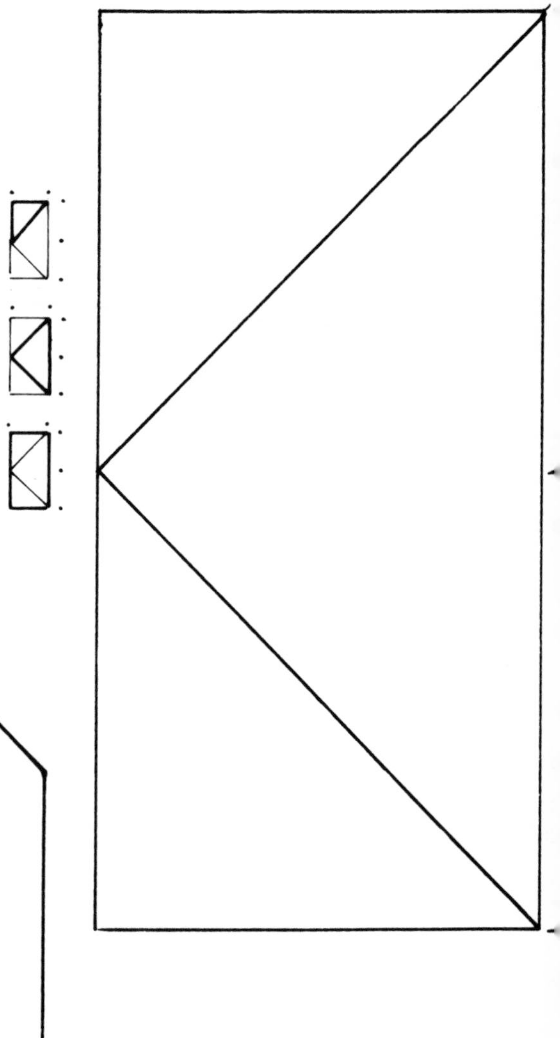

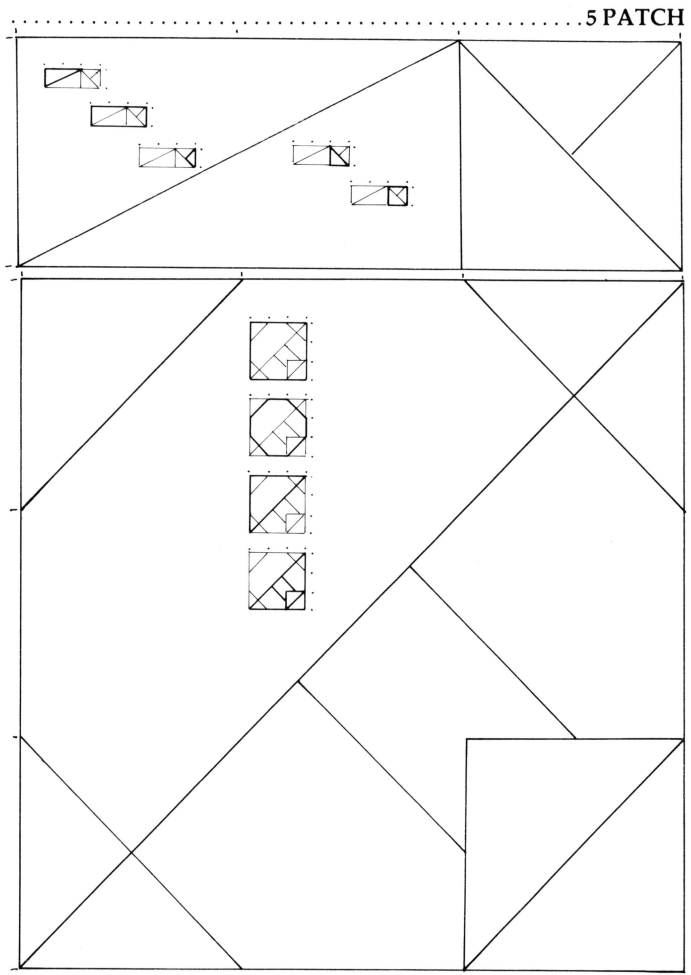

STAR . . . .

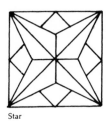
Star

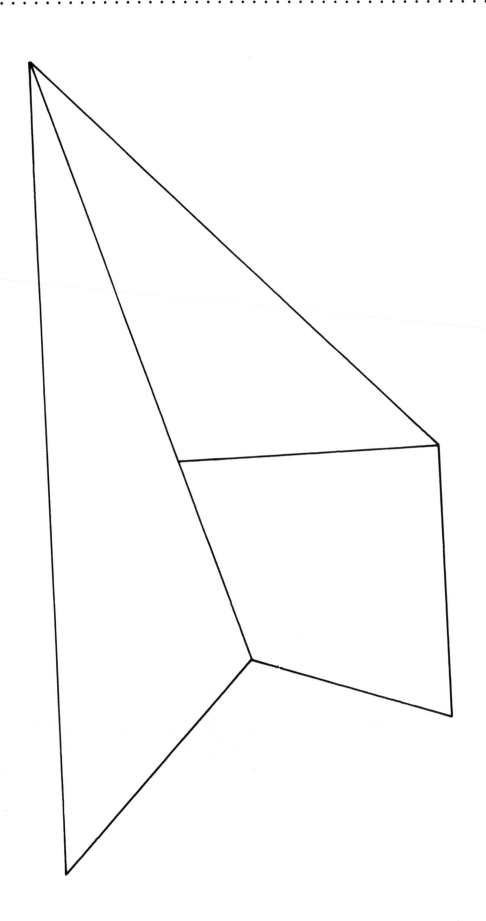

BEGINNERS

INTERMEDIATE

ADVANCED

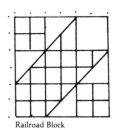

Basic 6

Road to California

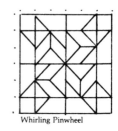

Lost Ship

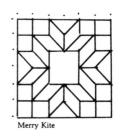

Whirling Pinwheel

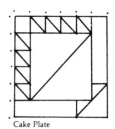

Railroad Block

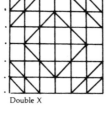

Puss-in-the-Corner

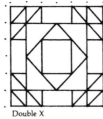

Double X

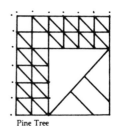

Merry Kite

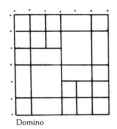

Cake Plate

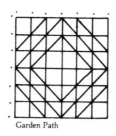

Double X

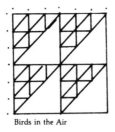

Cherry Basket

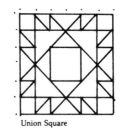

Pine Tree

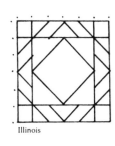

Domino

Garden Path

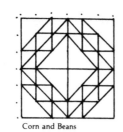

Birds in the Air

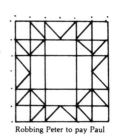

Union Square

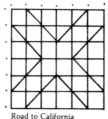

Illinois

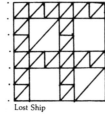

Stamp Basket

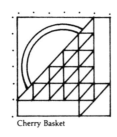

Corn and Beans

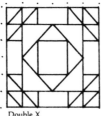

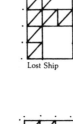

Robbing Peter to pay Paul

6 PATCH

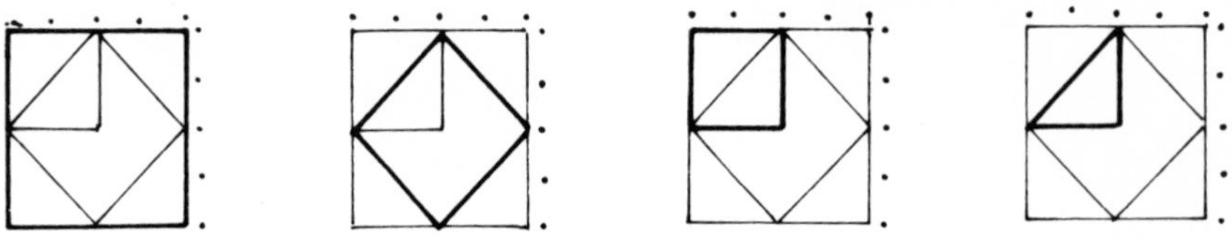

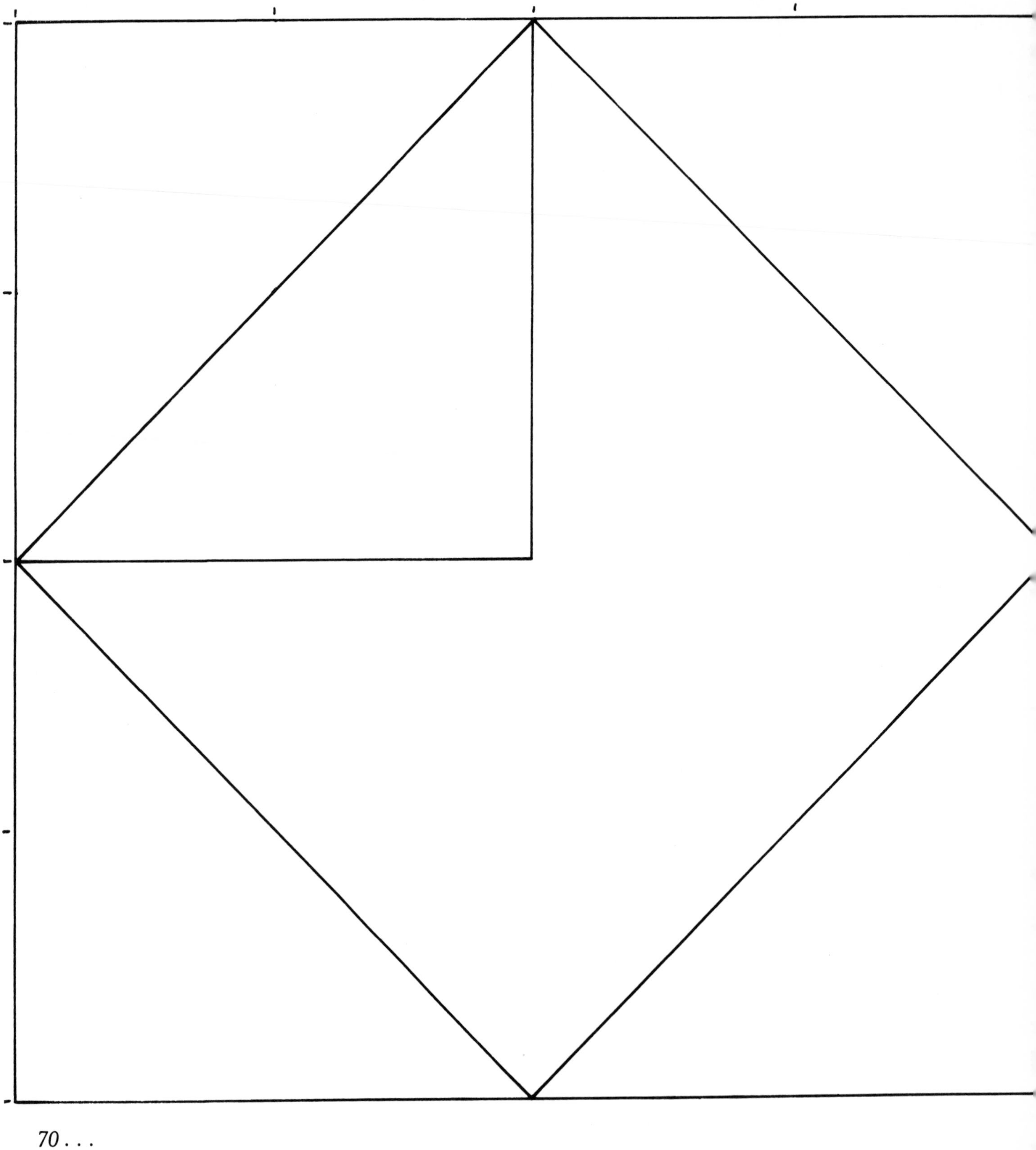

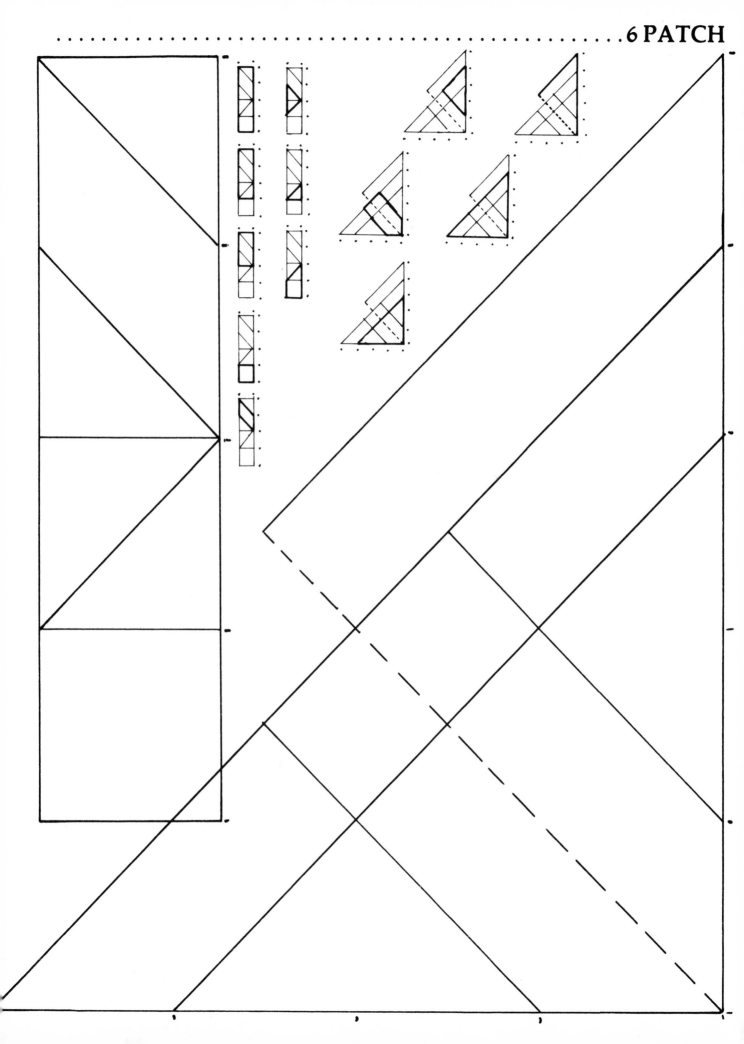

1 PATCH . . . .

Dresdin Plate

Blazing Star

8 Pointed Star

Star of LeMoine